CHAPEL HILL
AND
ELISHA MITCHELL
THE BOTANIST

Rogers McVaugh, Michael R. McVaugh, and Mary Ayers

THE BOTANICAL GARDEN FOUNDATION, Chapel Hill, N.C.
1996

Copyright © 1996
by The Botanical Garden Foundation

All rights reserved

ISBN 1-889065-00-5

Library of Congress Catalog Card Number 96-84919

This volume is identified as No. 1 of the Occasional Publications of the Chapel Hill Historical Society, and Contribution No. 1 from the North Carolina Botanical Garden. Publication was facilitated by financial aid from the Historical Society and from the Botanical Garden, to both of which the authors express their gratitude.

CONTENTS

Preface	1
Introduction	3
Mitchell and Schweinitz	6
Mitchell as a botanist	10
Botanical identification	18
Mitchell's botanical notes	29
Appendix A: Chapel Hill's topography and Mitchell's botanizing localities	64
Appendix B: The genesis of Map 1	70
Appendix C: An eclectic index to Mitchell's places and people	75
Appendix D: The numbered tracts shown on Map 1	83
Appendix E: The numbered lots in the village of Chapel Hill (Map 2)	94
Literature cited	107
Plant-names mentioned in the text	111
Personal names mentioned in the text	119
Map 1 and caption	inside back cover

PREFACE

The name of Elisha Mitchell is known chiefly because of his work as a geologist in North Carolina and his explorations in the mountainous western part of that State, which led ultimately to his death in 1857 on the highest peak, later named in his honor. His name is commemorated in the Elisha Mitchell Scientific Society and in its *Journal*, which began publication in 1884, and devoted its Centennial Issue (Volume 100, no. 2: [37]–81. 1984) to assessments of Mitchell's contributions in the sciences and in the humanities, to the University of North Carolina and to the State of North Carolina. His continuing scientific interests in chemistry and geology are well documented, as is his contribution toward building up for the university what was for the time among the best scientific libraries in the United States.

The centennial celebration of the founding of the Elisha Mitchell Scientific Socitety, held in 1983, included the delivery of serveral brief papers on aspects of Elisha Mitchell's scientific life in North Carolina – his chemistry, his geology, and his reading – based on his printed papers but also in part on his manuscript ledgers in the University of North Carolina library. Studying those ledgers made it clear that there was also a story to be told about a hitherto unknown side of Mitchell's scientific activity in Chapel Hill, his early fascination with botany, which has scarcely been noticed except for a paragraph in the same Centennial Issue of the Elisha Mitchell *Journal* (pp. 52–53). Two of us were well placed by our training as botanical taxonomist and historian of science, respectively, to explore that story. As we began to do so, however, it became obvious to us that a full account of Mitchell's botanizing would have to have a topographic dimension as well, and we soon found a professional surveyor with a thorough familiarity with Chapel Hill and its geography, who joined us in the research. Over the past half-dozen years our study has become a much broader one than we had originally envisaged, and we hope the result will be of some interest to a range of audiences – to those concerned with early American natural history, to those interested in the young University of North Carolina, and to those simply curious about what Chapel Hill was like nearly two hundred years ago.

In the preparation of this volume we have received generous assistance and suggestions from many sources. Above all, we are deeply grateful to the late Jane Summerell for her interest in and support for our study of her ancestor. Our long-continued search for old records in the office of the Register of Deeds in Hillsborough was greatly facilitated by the kindness of the staff and especially that of Virginia C. Forrest. Our thanks go to the staffs of the North Carolina Collection and the Southern Historical Collection of the University of North Carolina library, for their patience with our many requests, and for permission to reproduce certain documents as our Figures 1 and 2, and Map 2. We are happy to acknowledge the contribution made by Daniel G. Musser, without whose specialized knowledge the preparation of our new map would have been much more difficult. We thank Leo P. Bruederle, Joseph Ewan, E. A. Schuyler, and R. L. Stuckey, for assistance in tracking down Mitchell's botanical specimens. Many friends in Chapel Hill, especially Kevin Cherry, Mary McKee Felton, William Lanier Hunt, Charlotte Jones-Roe, J. R. Massey, Margie Pfaff, Albert E. Radford, Pearson Stewart, Peter S. White, and Sheldon White, contributed information, comments, suggestions and encouragement for which we are most grateful. Julia A. McVaugh read the entire manuscript and brought her very considerable editorial talent to our aid. Christiane Anderson, with her usual consummate devotion to the production of first quality books, saw our effort through the press.

Rogers McVaugh
Research Professor of Botany, UNC-CH

Michael R. McVaugh
Professor of History, UNC-CH

Mary Ayers
N. C. Registered Land Surveyor
Ayers Surveying Company, Chapel Hill

Chapel Hill, N.C., 30 June 1996

INTRODUCTION

Elisha Mitchell came to Chapel Hill in 1818, not long out of Yale, to teach mathematics at the University of North Carolina. Born in 1793, two years before the University opened its doors, he was young with a young man's enthusiasms. Chapel Hill was a very small village, still sometimes referred to in land deeds as the "village of the University." Much of the land in the vicinity was still uncleared, covered with a mature forest consisting largely of oaks and hickories. There were many springs on and along all sides of the "Hill," and small streams running down into two major creeks, one to the north and the other to the south. Before Mitchell had been long in residence, he began to spend many hours exploring the country near the University, looking at the native plants and identifying them. He continued to pursue this interest in botany vigorously at least until 1824, when other affairs began to preempt his time. He was made Professor of Chemistry, Mineralogy, and Geology, and he was forced by circumstances and his own ability into University administration. His major contribution to science was in geology, especially that of North Carolina, and in the botanical literature there are only a few incidental mentions of his name. Nevertheless, because of the intensity with which he pursued the subject for a few years, we think it worth describing his botanical activities in more detail.

In 1819, when Mitchell was beginning to think about active botanical work, the University of North Carolina bore little resemblance to the University of today. It was geographically isolated in what had been a wilderness less than seventy-five years before. The program of instruction was rigorous, but to modern eyes it was narrowly focused.[1] In 1819 the student body numbered 119. The senior faculty, which the preceding year had consisted of President Joseph Caldwell (also Professor of Moral Philosophy and Metaphysics), William Hooper (Professor of Ancient Languages), and Elisha Mitchell (Professor of Mathematics), was increased to five active members by the arrival of Denison Olmsted (Mitchell's classmate at Yale, and Professor of Chemistry), and Shepard K. Kollock (newly appointed Professor of Rhetoric).

Admission to the freshman class was predicated upon long training in Latin and Greek and little else. The freshman year in college included more Latin and Greek, antiquities and ancient geography, mathematics (arithmetic, algebra), modern geography, and English (grammar, composition, declamations, and theses). The sophomore year was much the same, including all the works of Horace and

---

[1]The discussion of the early days of the University has been drawn primarily from Battle's history of that institution (Battle, vol. 1, 1907).

Fig. 1. The "President's House" on village lot no. 2, as envisioned in a sketch made in the 1920s by Mitchell's granddaughter, Faith Summerell Chamberlain, and published in her book *Old Days in Chapel Hill* (Chapel Hill, N.C., 1926), p. 154. Published here by courtesy of the North Carolina Collection, University of North Carolina Library at Chapel Hill. The house was built for the first President of the University, Joseph Caldwell, but after about 1807 it was used as a dwelling for other faculty members. Elisha Mitchell lived there with his family for thirty-seven years (Battle, 1907, p. 253).

four books of Homer's *Iliad*. In the junior year there was no Latin or Greek, but there was advanced mathematics (including what are now called analytical geometry, calculus, plane and spherical trigonometry, and such practical operations as mensuration, surveying, and navigation); natural philosophy, which we would now call physics, was added, and English continued, including study of the great English authors. In the senior year there was no Latin, Greek, or pure mathematics, but for the first time there was natural science — including chemistry, mineralogy, geology, and philosophy of natural history. Under the heading of philosophy, the class studied moral philosophy, metaphysics, and the progress of metaphysical, ethical, and political philosophy. English this last year included logic, rhetoric, classics, composition, and declamation.

Much of what we know about Mitchell's activities during his first two decades in Chapel Hill comes from his jottings — arranged in no discernible order — preserved in a ledger in the Southern Historical Collection at the University of North Carolina at Chapel Hill, prefaced by the words, "For myself and Nobody else."[2] One of these jottings (p. 195), headed "Chapel Hill January 12th 1818," must have been set down almost immediately upon his arrival in the village, and outlines the program he first set himself as a newly fledged Professor of Mathematics:

> Plan of Studies for the Session. From the time of rising in the Morning till 9 o'clock — the Lessons of the Day. From 9 to 11, Vince's Fluxions

---

[2]Elisha Mitchell Papers, vol. 2 (hereafter EM2).

[= calculus]. From 12 to 2, Letters. Private. Recitation. Miscellanies. The lessons of the Day. From 2 to 4, Optics. From Prayers to bed Time, 1/2 an hour on Euclid. Locke, Language, Poetry, Religion &c.

In the summer of that first year in Chapel Hill, Mitchell seems to have adopted a more self-conscious introspection, opening a new section of his ledger in French with the date "Septembre 9me 1818," a heading in large letters, "Compte Ouvert," and the subhead "De Mes études, mes pensées — De mon être" (EM2, p. 2). There follows a short entry in English, on mathematics, but the first extended thoughts come on "Mé[r]credi, Juillet 28me 1819."[3] Again he was preoccupied with ordering his time, but now a new priority is apparent:

> Je voudrai une exact repartition que chaque étude aurais ses heures. Je note ici l'ordre des travaux de la journée.
> Premierement. Je me leverai au lever du soleil et après les matins Je m'appliquerai aux les Mathematiques — principalement à l'algèbre de Euler aux onze heures — Je ne toucherai pas aucune livre des belles lettres.
> Secondement. De la récitation au diné Je lirai les journaux. J'écrirai ce compte celui ci et les lettres etc.
> Troisièmement. Après diner au quatre heures la langue Espagnol et la botanie. Je ne toucherai pas aucune livre Anglais à moins que les livres botaniques.
> Quatrièment. Du cinque heures au soir botanie, Belles lettres et récréation.
> [Cinquièmement omitted]
> Sixièment. La soirée. Les leçons du demain — Histoire des Greques.
> Septièmèment. Samedi aù Matin Latin et Greque. Soir Hebreu.
> Juillet. La soirée passée j'etois à le docteur Caldwell ax [aux?] neuf heures et demie. Apres mon retour je lisais l'histoire de Greece par Mitford. Ce matin je me levais aux sept heures et demie. J'étais Malade et je lisais 80 lignes dans la traité de Cicero sur la veillesse.

There ends the personal journal. Twenty months after arriving in Chapel Hill, Mitchell had apportioned a part of every afternoon (except of course Sunday, and perhaps Saturday) to botany, at the same time not neglecting his mathematics, his general reading, the study of Greek history, and of the Spanish, Latin, Greek, and Hebrew languages. We do not know how well he was able to keep to his intended regime. Certainly in the two or three years after this he was so much occupied with botany that he may well have spent most of his afternoons on it, perhaps at the expense of the Spanish language. While he did not record whether he thought of his morning stint of Eulerian algebra as a task or as something to anticipate with pleasure, we do know from his notes and letters how much he enjoyed in these early days getting back to his beloved botany — his "studia dilecta nimium neglecta," as he once said.[4]

---

[3] We have not attempted to correct the errors in Mitchell's spelling of French.

[4] EM2, p. 151; see also below, p. 53. In this account of Mitchell's botanizing we will sometimes quote his words without attribution, but all such passages can be found in the text we supply of his botanical notes, pp. 29–63.

MITCHELL AND SCHWEINITZ

It seems likely that Mitchell's early interest in botany was aroused or at least stimulated by his acquaintance with Lewis David de Schweinitz (1780–1835). It is perhaps not coincidental that Mitchell's planned allotment of time to botany was recorded by him during the summer of 1819, near the time when he first visited Schweinitz in Salem. Schweinitz was a remarkable man: he was a theologian and the administrator of the church estates of the Moravian brethren in North Carolina, resident in Salem from 1812 to 1821 and thereafter in Bethlehem, Pennsylvania. He was also a botanist, known for his revisionary studies in *Viola* (Schweinitz, 1822) and *Carex* (Schweinitz, 1824; Schweinitz and Torrey, 1826), and especially for his pioneering work in mycology. He has been the subject of a very considerable body of biographical material, for the botanical part of which the reader may consult Stafleu and Cowan (1985), or Shear and Stevens (1921). As Schweinitz informed John Torrey, when he first came to Carolina he "almost exclusively attached [himself] to the Fungi" and formed a collection of about 1500 species, all from the vicinity of Salem; after a trip to Europe in 1817–1818, he "pretty zealously" turned his attention to mosses, liverworts, lichens, and freshwater algae. When he wrote to Torrey on June 24, 1820, his herbarium included nearly 6000 plants, including what he called Phaenogams (i.e., flowering plants). As a postscript to the same letter, he added: "By the Rev. C. F. Denke lately established in our vicinity the botanical fraternity of North Carolina has obtained a valuable recruit & now forms a quadro. Rev. Jacob Van Vleck, C. F. Denke & myself here, and Prof. Mitchell at Chapel Hill. I am afraid there is no other soul in the state" (Shear and Stevens, pp. 125, 126). Neither of the other men that Schweinitz mentioned was primarily a naturalist. Van Vleck (1751–1831) had come to Salem with Schweinitz in 1812 as pastor of Salem, and was made bishop in 1815; Denke (1775–1838), a Moravian missionary, was pastor at Hope (1820–1822) and at Friedberg (1822–1831), and continued botanical collecting in Salem after Schweinitz left (Clewell, 1902).

Mitchell's ledger contains notes in his hand (EM2, p. 221) that shed light on the state of the countryside about Salem at this time. Not dated, they are written in the present tense:

> Bethany 33 dwelling houses at the utmost. Bethabara 16. Salem 54. The Wachovia tract was purchased of Lord Granville in 1753. Settlement begun by 12 young men who came on to make a clearing in 1754. They were from Pennsylvania from whence most of the Brethren in this state came. First house built in Salem 1766. There were constant removals from Beth-

abara till 1772, when the fiscal concerns of the two places were separated and Salem became a distinct town. It was never intended that Bethabara should be the chief and permanent settlement. Salem is a very little south of the center of the Wachovia tract. Bethany was settled about the same time with Salem. Charlestown or Bagg-town has 8 dwelling houses. Martinsville 5. Greenesborough 30. Salisbury 100 at the utmost.

Mitchell had visited Salem in 1819, and for a time thereafter he depended on Schweinitz to help him with plant-identifications. Writing on September 29 of that year, Mitchell explained apologetically that he had not yet received the copy of Frederick Pursh's *Flora Americae Septentrionalis* that he hoped to make his field guide:

> As to my progress in Botany I am ashamed to tell you how little I have done. But indeed with my present help it is so discouraging to attempt to determine a plant that I have done next to nothing. I have a copy of Pursh on the way here from New York which ought to have been here long ago and I was promising myself that I should make...advances when it arrives but I now begin to feel that I shall do little this season, but by next spring by which time the books I have ordered from Europe will have come to hand I purpose to recommence with new vigour.[1]

Evidently his copy of Pursh arrived as expected during the winter of 1819–1820, as he constantly referred to it during the field-season of 1820.

For a man who later described himself as one "not much given to enthusiasm on any subject," Mitchell's inclination toward botany now ran remarkably free, leading him dangerously close to what we might think was enthusiasm. Especially from 1820 to 1822, at least in the spring, he made almost daily excursions to study and collect the local plants as they came into flower, and he continued to refer his occasional problems to Salem. On June 14 [1820] there are entries in his ledger — "*Stylosanthes hispida erecta* Mr. Schweinitz," and "*Lycopodium apodum* Mr. Schweinitz, Pursh" — indicating that Schweinitz had provided the primary identifications. On the same day he noted, "(Hepaticae) *Marchantia polymorpha*. Mere guesswork from the plant being called Liverwort. To be sent to Mr. Schweinitz." We suppose that Schweinitz had early encouraged Mitchell to send him botanical specimens, and a "Catalogue of Plants to be sent to Mr. Schweinitz" in the ledger (p. 111) was probably written in 1819 or perhaps 1820. Although it is followed without a break by discussion dated May 6, 1822, the relative botanical naiveté that is evident in the "Catalogue" suggests someone at the beginning of his botanizing in the South, rather than the same person who had given it two years of regular attention:

> A plant of the Class Syngenesia believed a *Gnaphalium* — March 5.
> A Plant thought to be *Draba verna*. Found in low cultivated grounds.
> Another of the Class Tetrydynamia. Associated with the last. Perhaps also a *Draba*.
> Another of the same Class. In the field N.E of Scotts Hole.

---

[1]Mitchell to Schweinitz, September 29, 1819; Academy of Natural Sciences (photostat in Southern Historical Collection, University of North Carolina Library).

> A *Salix* found going out of flower E of Scotts Hole. Leaves to be examined.
> I am not satisfied about the *Stellaria* I have. Tis in abundance along Bollings Creek.
> Question is the plum near Mr. Lewis's the *Prunus chicasa* ———
> I have a *Ranunculus* I do not find in the books ——— One flowered More [ends here]
> March 28. Another Tetradyamous [sic] plant — flowers yellow. N.B. The pedate [illegible].
> April 8. A syngenesious plant believed an *Erigeron*.

There seems no way to determine whether or not the "Catalogue" and the accompanying plants were ever sent.

Mitchell continued to send plants to Schweinitz for determination in the season of 1821, including the "elegant specimens [of *Viola sagittata*] found at Chapel-Hill by Professor Mitchell" that were acknowledged the next year (Schweinitz, 1822, p. 56). By the fall, however, he had already been informed of Schweinitz's plan to move to Pennsylvania and was disconsolate. In a letter of October 5 he wrote, "Who will now correct my mistakes in Phenogamy and who will unlock to me the more hidden arcana of the science of botany?" Nevertheless, on 20 October, in spite of the imminent move (Schweinitz planned to leave about November 20; see Shear and Stevens, 1921, p. 153), Mitchell sent him for identification 16 specimens "gathered last Wednesday morning"; 170 specimens mounted ("wafered on sheets") to be returned; and 42 unmounted ("loose") numbered specimens.[2] Evidently Schweinitz made an effort to finish the identifications before he left, as Mitchell's letter of November 8 acknowledged the receipt that same day of a trunk (presumably containing the specimens) and also a copy of Bridel's *Muscologia* that Schweinitz had offered him. The Bridel was so exciting to Mitchell that he went out the same day to collect mosses. In his letter of acknowledgment he mentioned sending mosses to Schweinitz and said, among other things, "My wife has been some of the time laughing with me at your very amusing observations on my plants and the rest of it laughing at me for the eagerness with which I entered upon the business of devouring poor Mr. Bridel."[3]

Schweinitz continued his interest in botany after leaving Salem, and he wrote at least one letter to Mitchell requesting help in obtaining certain interesting plants from North Carolina,[4] but communication between the two men must have been interrupted at the time of the move, and undoubtedly became more difficult afterward. It seems odd, for example, that in 1828 when Mitchell undertook to compile a little synopsis of the 21 local species of *Carex* that he had identified, he seems not to have been aware of Schweinitz's publications on the same genus in 1824 and 1826. The intensity of his interest in botany may have declined after Schweinitz's departure, although it is clear that the subject long continued to

---

[2]Mitchell to Schweinitz, October 20, 1821; Academy of Natural Sciences (photostat in Southern Historical Collection, University of North Carolina Library). See also EM2, p. 184 (October 16, 1821).

[3]Mitchell to Schweinitz, November 8, 1821; Academy of Natural Sciences (photostat in Southern Historical Collection, University of North Carolina Library). See also EM2, p. 184 (November 8, 1821).

[4]Schweinitz to Mitchell, November 13, 1822; Elisha Mitchell papers, Southern Historical Collection, University of North Carolina Library.

intrigue him. In the years that followed, his fascination with the subject was manifested, not in annual collecting, but in brief surges of interest that led to special studies of certain difficult groups of plants, by way of furthering his understanding of the local species.

The weakening of Mitchell's botanical fervor was no doubt partly caused by the deprivation of the stimulus of Schweinitz's presence in Salem only eighty miles away, but other factors were also involved. By chance, the departure of Schweinitz coincided with Mitchell's increasing involvement in University affairs. In 1824 he was made acting president of the University while President Caldwell was in Europe, and when his colleague Denison Olmsted resigned in 1825, Mitchell was appointed to the chair of Chemistry, Mineralogy, and Geology, a position that he held for the rest of his life. The new position channeled his enthusiasm for the natural sciences in a new direction, as did his appointment in the same year to lead the North Carolina Geological Survey. Not long thereafter he was made bursar of the University, with responsibility for most administrative matters, both instructional and fiscal, as well as for disciplinary control of about 100 students. In addition to his weekday duties in school, Mitchell officiated as chaplain at prayers five evenings a week, preached Sunday sermons, and was otherwise a full-time participant in the religious side of university life, which at that time was taken for granted for all staff and students. He must have been a very busy man, and it is little wonder that botanizing was pushed to one side for the rest of his life.

MITCHELL AS A BOTANIST

From Mitchell's notes it is apparent that his principal concerns with botany were floristic; he wanted to be able to recognize all the local plants. At the same time, he was also interested in what is often called phenology — that is to say, the periodicity of flowering and fruiting with respect to climate. The notes dealing with botanical excursions in Orange County around Chapel Hill and as far afield as Hillsborough, the county seat twelve miles away, mention more than 350 species of plants — the great majority noted during the season of 1820, but others, especially spring-flowering species, from 1821 to 1825. Seldom is a name mentioned more than once, except when he wished to compare dates of flowering from year to year, or when he was not satisfied with some earlier identification. Pretty clearly he was consciously compiling a local floristic list, and mentioning only such plants as were new to the list. Many, of course, were new not only to the *Flora Mons-Sacelliensis* (a term he once coined, from Lat. *sacellum*, meaning shrine or chapel), but also quite unfamiliar to him, who had lived his early life in New England.

In a letter to Schweinitz (June 1821) Mitchell reflected his floristic interest, at the same time expressing a thoughtful wish that was not to be fulfilled for 121 years (with the publication of the first volume of S. F. Blake's monumental *Geographical Guide to the Floras of the World*): "I'll tell you what botanists need badly. It is a book describing all the floras that have ever been published with great exactness — stating what are their several merits and in what degree they will be useful to one who is pursuing the study."[1]

It is clear that Mitchell became botanically well informed and quite capable of tracking down an unknown plant in the floristic works of his day, which was no mean feat. On the other hand he was not primarily a botanist. Where critical knowledge of a particular plant-group was needed, he often expressed doubt about the correctness of his identifications. He had been trained in science at Yale, but it is not at all certain that he studied botany there. About 1820, when he was first writing to Schweinitz, he seemed less sure of himself than in later seasons when he had practiced using Pursh, Elliott, and other floras. He very probably knew some plants by sight when he came to North Carolina, though surely he was unfamiliar at first with the flora of the deep Southeast. By the summer of 1821, however, he was able to send to Schweinitz a plausible list of the Coastal Plain plants he had seen on a recent trip to Fayetteville: "I found in flower *Utricularia*

---

[1] Mitchell to Schweinitz, June 1821; Academy of Natural Sciences (photostat in Southern Historical Collection, University of North Carolina Library).

subulata, Pinguicula elatior, Lupinus perennis and *villosa, Chaptalia tomentosa, Erigeron nudicaule, Hopaea [Symplocos] tinctoria, Styrax glabrum, Podalyria villosa, Viburnum nudum, Helonias angustifolia, Andromeda nitida, Viola digitata, Sarracenia purpurea* and *flava* and saw some others which the rain and the hurry I was in prevented me from ascertaining." He continued, "As Mrs. Mitchell is now away I dry but few [plants] and those few but badly preserved. I hope she will soon return in order that Botany may flourish."[2] It is not clear just what part Mrs. Mitchell took in the plant-drying; perhaps he dried the plants over her cook-stove, which was unused during her absence.

In order to document his botanical observations, Mitchell must have collected and preserved a considerable number of conventional herbarium specimens. In early notes made in March 1820 he noted several times, in reference to particular plants, "Dried the blossoms," or simply "Dried." As recorded above, between 1819 and 1821 he sent numerous specimens to Schweinitz for naming; a shipment including more than 200 specimens was sent to Schweinitz in October 1821 and was returned a month later, just before the latter's departure from Salem. We do not know the fate of the majority of Mitchell's plant-specimens, including those returned by Schweinitz in 1821 and any others he may have preserved. Personal herbaria like his were many in the early nineteenth century, and were usually carefully preserved, so we cannot explain why the bulk of Mitchell's plants did not survive. Perhaps his collection was discarded as waste paper after his accidental death, or perhaps he neglected it in his later life as he turned to other pursuits, or even discarded it himself.

James Mears (1981, p. 158) stated that the Academy of Natural Sciences of Philadelphia had acquired Mitchell specimens from two sources, the herbarium of L. D. von Schweinitz and that of Charles Wilkins Short (1794–1863). Short was an able student of the flora of Kentucky and adjacent areas; he was professor and later dean at Transylvania University, and was most active from about 1825 to 1835. His herbarium of some 15,000 specimens was acquired by the Academy in 1964 (Stafleu and Cowan, 1985). We have not confirmed any connection between Mitchell and Short, nor have we seen any specimens that Mitchell may have given to Short, but it is established that Schweinitz saved a significant number of the plant specimens that Mitchell sent him. Schweinitz, it will be remembered, in his monograph on *Viola* (Schweinitz, 1822), complimented Mitchell on the quality of the specimens he had sent from Chapel Hill; the same specimens are still preserved with others from the personal herbarium of Schweinitz, now at the Academy of Natural Sciences. R. L. Stuckey (1979, p. 12), in his list of the types in the Schweinitz herbarium, published a photograph of Mitchell's specimens of *Viola sagittata*, without mentioning the collector, but showing in the picture the handwritten locality "Chapel Hill" associated with the plants. In the same publication (p. 33) Stuckey listed among the type-specimens at the Academy that of *Carex sempervirens* (Schweinitz, 1824, p. 70), a Mitchell collection made at Hillsborough. During a recent visit to the Academy, one of us (MRMcV) confirmed that the specimens of *Viola sagittata* are still there, and confirmed at the same time, to our considerable surprise and pleasure, the presence of Mitchell's specimens of *Lindera ("Laurus") melissifolia*, his "shrub in the pond," his report of which has not been credited in modern times (see below, pp. 25–26).

---

[2]Mitchell to Schweinitz, June 1821; Academy of Natural Sciences (photostat in Southern Historical Collection, University of North Carolina Library).

Finally, in three manuscript enumerations of the plants in his herbarium, Schweinitz listed specimens belonging to a total of at least twenty-eight species, all presumably collected by Mitchell: one from the Peaks of Otter (Virginia), the others with the locality "Chapel Hill" except for two labelled merely "Orange County." Other similar entries may have been overlooked in our necessarily brief survey. The three lists of the herbarium are preserved in three ledgers in Collection 137 of the Archives of the Academy. One (137 #5) is dated 1822, or shortly after Schweinitz removed to Pennsylvania from North Carolina; one (#7) is dated 1824; and a third (#12) is undated but is probably from the early 1830s, as it includes collections made by Christoph Weigelt in Surinam ca. 1827–1828. The successive lists were not only enlarged but emended as Schweinitz changed his mind or received new information. Following is a list of the names that presumably represent Schweinitz's more mature judgments on Mitchell's plants, taken from the "1830s" ledger (#12) and arranged in the order in which they appear there. Notes on names for the same plants in the 1822 list are included if it seems desirable, and if the citation in the later list is incomplete. We have not attempted to provide modern names for the species; with few exceptions, the generic names are those in use today.

Justicia brachiata (12:8); Monarda clinopodia, Peaks of Otter (12:5); Paspalum strictum (12:24); Agrostis brevifolia/spadicea LvS (12:25); Spermacoce tenuior vix — an prioris [= diodina] (12:43) [this was Spermacoce tenuis of 5:26]; Cornus caroliniana LS (12:47) [this was listed as "Cornus didyma Nobis. Anonym." in 5:28, but the new name seems not to have been published]; Phlox acuminata (5:34 [the only reference to Chapel Hill]); Azalea canescens (12:58); Nicandra physaloides (12:61); Bumelia (in both #5 and #12); Vitis riparia (5:36); Sabbatia chloroides (12:55); Viola sagittata (5:39); Asclepias verticillata-angustifolia LvS. . . an linifolia Spr. (12:71) [this was listed as "Asclepias Mitchelii Nobis" in 5:39, but neither new name seems to have been published]; Bupleurum rotundifolium (12:73); Trillium nervosum (12:91); Viburnum pubescens (5:45); Laurus melisoides Ell. (12:99) [this was Laurus diospyros of 5:55]; Andromeda nitida (12:100); Asarum arifolium (12:112); Eupatorium parviflorum Elliott (12:176); Liatris graminifolia (12:177); Baccharis _____? (12:179); Baccharis glomieruliflora (12:179) [neither this nor the preceding is listed in #5]; Solidago sorbifolia Ell. (12:186) [this was Solidago virgata of 5:105]; Eclipta ("Eclipsa") (12:189) [this was Eclipsa erecta of 5:107]; Helianthus tomentosus Ell. (12:192); Silphium laciniatum (12:193).

When Schweinitz wrote (on a specimen-label or in one of his catalogs) the name of a species that he believed was new to science, it was his practice to write the generic name followed by the specific epithet that he proposed to give it, concluding with his initials "LvS" or with the word Nobis — that is to say, "of us." This was the editorial "us" much used in such circumstances in the eighteenth and nineteenth centuries to designate a "new species" (for many examples of this use by Schweinitz, see Stuckey, 1979). Thus *Asclepias mitchelii* Nobis in the above list meant "our *Asclepias mitchelii*," or, as one might say today, "my *Asclepias mitchelii*." Initials following the Latin name are intended to show the same connection between the author and the name of the species. It may be supposed that *Agrostis spadicea* LvS, *Cornus caroliniana* LS, and *Asclepias angustifolia* LvS were all names that Schweinitz intended at the time to publish as new, on the basis of Mitchell's specimens from Chapel Hill. It is clear that although Mitchell learned much and benefited greatly from his association with Schweinitz during the years the latter lived in Salem, he repaid at least a part of the debt by contributing more than a few items that helped Schweinitz to build up a broad picture of the flora of North Carolina and the surrounding territory, and eventually to bring to publication his *Synopsis Plantarum Americanarum*, which still exists in manuscript at the Academy (Stuckey, 1979, p. 47).

In the years after the departure of Schweinitz from North Carolina, Mitchell shared his botanical knowledge, and at least some specimens, with Moses Ashley Curtis (1808–1872), who first came to North Carolina (Wilmington) as a tutor in 1830, became an Episcopal minister, first visited Hillsborough in 1835, and settled there in 1841 (Berkeley and Berkeley, 1986). Curtis botanized in the Wilmington area from the time of his arrival there, and continued actively in this pursuit. He began to correspond with Mitchell (among many others) on botanical matters, and on at least one trip, in 1836, he stopped in Chapel Hill to visit with Mitchell. By the 1840s he was undoubtedly the state's best-known botanist. In his survey of the woody plants of North Carolina, published after Mitchell's death, Curtis acknowledged (Curtis, 1860, p. xv): "The Rev. Dr. Mitchell, during one period of his Professorship at our University, was an assiduous cultivator of Botanical Science, and had made a considerable collection of specimens, which he generously shared with Dr. Schweinitz and myself. I am indebted to him for several species which had otherwise been yet unknown to our North-Carolina Flora. A species of Carex, named after him, commemorates his devotion to the beautiful science." In the same paper Curtis admitted *Benzoin melissaefolium* and *Euonymus atropurpureus* to the state flora partly on Mitchell's authority, and in a later publication (Curtis, 1867) he included on the same authority the same two species (pp. 47 and 15, respectively) and six others: *Aphyllon uniflorum* (p. 38), *Cardamine ludoviciana* (p. 10), *Centaurea calcitrapa* (p. 33), *Ellisia nyctelea* (p. 42), *Eupatorium parviflorum* (p. 27), and *Vernonia fasciculata* (p. 26).

The *Carex* to which Curtis referred was *C. mitchelliana*, which he himself had named in Mitchell's honor in 1843 (Curtis, 1843, p. 84). He based the name on a plant collected in Chatham County in 1835, and it is entirely possible (though we do not know and Curtis did not make it clear) that Mitchell had collected specimens — Chatham County virtually abuts Chapel Hill — and shown them to Curtis when the latter visited or established himself in the Piedmont. As Dr. Leo P. Bruederle has kindly informed us, however, Chester Dewey reported (Dewey, 1845) only two years after *Carex mitchelliana* was published that the plant had been discovered by Curtis himself. Whether Dewey had simply drawn this conclusion from the language of Curtis's paper is still unclear. Unfortunately, no typespecimen of *C. mitchelliana* has been located, in spite of assiduous searches in the early part of the twentieth century by several interested parties.

The primary herbarium of Curtis, rich in fungi, was acquired by the Farlow Herbarium (Harvard University), and other Curtis specimens are reported to exist in the herbaria of Brown University, the New York Botanical Garden, the Academy of Natural Sciences (Philadelphia), and the U.S. National Herbarium. We are not aware of the existence of any of Mitchell's specimens in these herbaria, except for those at the Academy of Natural Sciences, among the Schweinitz *reliquiae*.

The Elisha Mitchell that Moses Curtis would have come to know in the late 1830s was a scientist very different from the unformed young professor of mathematics who had come down from Connecticut in 1818 and discovered a taste for botany. Taking over Olmsted's chair (and its responsibility for the state geological survey) in 1825 would have put pressure on him to concentrate most of his time on geology; so also would he have been constrained by his own intellectual limits. Mitchell never learned German and as a result did not make a serious effort to keep up with the scientific literature in that language. He built up a fine library in chemistry for the period down to about 1830 while French scientists were preeminent in the subject, but he seems to have lost interest in chemistry at the moment when leadership in its study began to pass to Germany (with the beginnings of organic chemistry in the 1820s). Geology, however, was decidedly an English science in the 1820s and 1830s.

Mitchell's new responsibilities to his students and to the state also oriented him toward viewing science as providing practical advantage rather than as satisfying intellectual curiosity. The year-long course that he gave in "Chemistry, Geology, Mineralogy, Botany, and Zoology" placed most emphasis on geology, which might profit agricultural and mining interests alike, and he prepared a detailed textbook on this subject for the use of his students (Mitchell, 1842). For "Natural History" he drew up a much briefer printed syllabus that helps us realize Mitchell's matured concept of botany and what it has to offer. We have seen two copies of this syllabus — one formerly the property of a student in the 1830s, the other of a student twenty years later — which prove to be different printings of an identical text, suggesting that Mitchell's lectures, once codified, did not evolve ([Mitchell], n.d.).

Natural History, the syllabus says, identifies ("ascertains"), classifies, and describes the different substances that occur in the three kingdoms of Natural History: Animal, Vegetable, and Mineral. "It is our practice," the text continues, "to make one of the kingdoms of nature (the Mineral) an object of attention for a considerable time, whilst we devote but a single lecture to each of the others; and these for the purpose of communicating a knowledge of the *methods* of Natural History, as much as with reference to the sciences of Botany and Zoology themselves." The botanical lecture, which Mitchell gave first, defined the science's goal as "principally to enable us to determine the particular *species* to which a given vegetable belongs." Given such a limited objective, it is not hard to understand why the lecture ended as follows:

As part of a liberal education, the study of Botany is to be defended chiefly on the ground that it affords an excellent exercise to the mental powers, generates habits of accurate observation, and furnishes a source of elegant and innocent recreation and amusement ([Mitchell], n.d., p. 8).

Mitchell's own abandonment of botanical activity may have been forced upon him by the demands of his new duties, but also he evidently found it difficult to justify a place for the study of botany in a university curriculum, in an increasingly practical age. In the early nineteenth century in America, most botanists (as Mitchell understood the term) were amateurs of plants — men for the most part — who earned their living in other ways. Many were medical doctors, or lawyers, or clergymen. As has recently been emphasized by Elizabeth Keeney (1992) in her study of amateur botanists ("botanizers") of the period, there were very few strictly scientific jobs, and it was not until mid-century that "a significant number of individuals were able to make a living at being knowledgeable" (p. 5).

What little Mitchell did tell his students about botany was already beginning to sound a little old-fashioned in 1830. Half of his lecture on the subject, as given in the syllabus, was devoted to explaining the sexual system of Linnaeus. He acknowledged that Antoine-Laurent de Jussieu had devised a system — in 1789, though Mitchell does not give the date — in which the whole vegetable kingdom was divided into one hundred families, "grouped together according to their natural affinities"; but he did not seem to see the exciting possibilities in this, saying merely, "the Linnaean system is the most convenient for the beginner" ([Mitchell], n.d., p. 7). In this respect Mitchell was still back in the eighteenth century, thinking of botany as merely plant-identification, at a time when the artificial Linnaean system had been largely superseded in science by the natural systems of de Jussieu and A. P. de Candolle.

To be sure, plant-identification based primarily on the convenient Linnaean system long remained popular as a subject for schools, academies, and private students. *Familiar Lectures on Botany*, by Almira H. Lincoln (Phelps), went through more than twenty editions between 1829 and 1864. It was aimed primarily at beginners in botany, and stressed the ease of identification by the Linnaean method, but from the beginning it gave lip service to the plant-families of the natural system. In the preface to the edition of 1853 the author expressed her agreement with William Darlington, "one of the first botanists of the age,"[3] who had written her as follows:

> I entirely concur with you in considering the *Linnaean method* as the easiest and most agreeable guide to the *first steps* of the learner, and would always so employ it. But as it only introduces one to what may be called a *speaking acquaintance* with plants, — merely enabling the student to *call them by name* when he meets with them, without teaching any thing of their real *character*, or presenting any inducement to inquire after their relations, — I incline to think that all those who wish to make any substantial progress in the knowledge of the vegetable creation, should pay an early attention to those essential features and characteristics which enable the attentive observer to group kindred plants into *natural families*. There is a gratification in tracing the *affinities* between kindred individuals, quite equal to the pleasure of detecting the *discrepancies* which serve to distinguish them; and it is the intelligent contemplation of *both* these aspects of the floral kingdom which constitutes the delight of the *true Botanist*." (Phelps, 1853, p. 4)

Mitchell seems never to have progressed much beyond Darlington's first stage, that of being able to call the plants by name. Apparently he remained oblivious to the advances that had been going on steadily for many years, and accelerating since 1800, in the subjects of plant anatomy, nutrition and growth, the cell theory,

---

[3]William Darlington (1782–1863) — a native of Chester County, Pennsylvania, the author of an admirable flora of that county (*Flora Cestrica*, 1837) and valuable memorials of William Baldwin, John Bartram, and Humphry Marshall (1843–1849) — was an M.D. (Pennsylvania, 1804), a world traveler, a linguist who handled French, German, Spanish, and Latin well, a public servant, a banker, and not least of all a botanist and historian. Mrs. Lincoln was not far off in her opinion of him, as expressed in 1851. See Harshberger, 1899, pp. 134–143.

plant sexuality, the alternation of generations, and reproductive biology — much of which, to be sure, was written in the German he could not read. In Darlington's sense, Mitchell never went beyond his early enthusiasm for identification to become a "true Botanist." His concept of what he called "botany" seems to have included little more than identification and floristics (his avocation), so that his students could scarcely have been aware of the contemporary dynamic growth of plant sciences in other directions. One wonders if this distinction is still observed at one of our major universities, where they currently maintain a joint department of Botany and Plant Sciences!

Inasmuch as Mitchell still had occasion for botanical reflection in the 1830s, it was with aims quite different both from those that are apparent in his early descriptive botanical notes, and from those Darlington had in mind. In 1833 the University faculty began to publish a short-lived newspaper, the *Harbinger*, and its second number included a contribution from H. B. Croom of New Bern, North Carolina, that described at length a plant that he called "gama grass." Croom gave most of his attention to deciding whether the plant should be called *Tripsacum dactyloides* or *T. monostachyon*, though he did comment (relatively briefly) on the possible economic advantages that would come from its cultivation. Mitchell himself probably oversaw the publication of Croom's contribution to the *Harbinger*, for he took the opportunity to follow it with a long commentary of his own in the same issue, praising the grass's economic potential:

> The individual who offers these few remarks to the readers of the Harbinger, is not much given to enthusiasm on any subject; but in regard to the Gama Grass, is sanguine in the expectation and belief that a vast addition will be made by it to the numbers, wealth and comforts of the population of North-Carolina.[4]

The more purely scientific problem of determining the grass's exact species, which clearly fascinated Croom, no longer held the interest for Mitchell that it once had; taxonomy had given way to agriculture in his concerns.

In fact it was now the intelligent amateur — Croom — who manifested the passion for plant identification and floristics that Mitchell had originally shown. Croom had graduated from the University in 1817, and so probably had never heard a lecture from Mitchell. He subsequently read law, and entered the General Assembly of North Carolina in 1828; two years later he resigned to attend to new family properties in Florida. Both in Florida and in North Carolina, however, botanizing was his true avocation, as it had been the young Mitchell's. In 1833, with Dr. Harris Loomis, Croom published a flora of New Bern, North Carolina (Mitchell owned a copy of the 1837 edition of this work). The next year, 1834, Croom published the first of a series of botanical articles in Benjamin Silliman's *American Journal of Science*. He established a friendship with John Torrey, and doubtless with Torrey's support was made a corresponding member of the New York Lyceum of Natural History. His paper on the taxonomy of *Sarracenia* was read before the society on September 5, 1826, and published the next year (Croom, 1837b). In the summer of 1837 he went to New York at least in part to see Torrey,

---

[4]*The Harbinger*, University of North Carolina, [Chapel Hill], No. 2 (Tuesday, September 3, 1833), p. 1. Mitchell signed his contributions to this and other numbers of the *Harbinger* with the letter "N."

and to finish the printing of a completely new edition of his flora of New Bern. The work was nearly complete when the lateness of the season made it imperative for him to return to the South, and he with his family were drowned in the wreck of the vessel that was carrying them home. Torrey saw the work through the press, and added a preface with an appreciation of Croom's work, saying among other things: "among the new plants discovered by Mr. Croom, and communicated to me, are…a noble new genus of Coniferae with the foliage of Taxus and a fruit as large as a nutmeg, which Dr. Arnott will shortly publish under the name of Torreya; and a very distinct new genus, to which I have given the name of Croomia, in honour of my departed friend" (Croom, 1837a, p. v).

Croom had been, before Moses Ashley Curtis, the most serious student of North Carolina botany. He had few competitors for the title — certainly not Elisha Mitchell, who as far as we know never published any strictly botanical book or paper. As early as the issue of the *Harbinger* that followed his remarks on the "gama grass," Croom had contributed "Memoranda of a Journey from New Bern to Raleigh" that reported the sequence of flowering species he had observed on a recent trip in passing from the Coastal Plain into the Piedmont (*Harbinger*, no. 3 [Tuesday, September 10, 1833], p. 1). He prefaced these "Memoranda" with a melancholy assessment of the state of botanical knowledge in the universities of the South: "I do not know that Botany is any where publicly taught in the Southern States. Elliott, and his zealous coadjutor McBride, are dead; Schweinitz and Leconte have abandoned the South."[5] In a still more plaintive footnote Croom remarked: "Prof. Eaton has just published at Albany the *sixth* edition of his 'Manual of Botany'. It is probable that not 50 copies of the six editions have been sold South of the Potomac." It bears out Croom's gloomy assessment that, while Mitchell's notes contain occasional references to Eaton and his *Manual*, at Mitchell's death there was no copy of the work among his books. Mitchell made no comment on this second article by Croom, but he must have recognized the accuracy of the impeachment, must indeed have recognized how it applied to him in particular. It is easy to imagine, in fact, that he must have felt a certain regret at having abandoned a subject he had once pursued so seriously. Sporadically during the later 1830s he made notes on an occasional botanical excursion, but he never really recaptured the whole-hearted commitment of his first years in Chapel Hill.

---

[5]Stephen Elliott (1771–1830) and James MacBride (1784–1817) had lived in Charleston. MacBride was a medical doctor who contributed observations on medical plants to Elliott's *Sketch*, and to whose memory the second volume of that work was dedicated. Schweinitz, as we have seen, had left Salem for Pennsylvania in 1821. John Eatton Leconte (1784–1860) and his less renowned brother Louis lived in their youth on the family plantation in Georgia; John, who was the author of several botanical monographs published between 1820 and 1828, entered the U.S. Army about 1817, resigned his commission in 1832 or 1833, and thereafter lived in New York or Philadelphia (Harshberger, 1899, pp. 149–151).

BOTANICAL IDENTIFICATION

The botanical observations made by Mitchell in his ledger are for the most part neither new nor profound, but they are still interesting from a botanical point of view because they set forth in considerable detail the steps that were necessary in order to identify an unknown plant from the contemporary literature, and they show how difficult and laborious it was to do this. At the same time, of course, the notes enable us to share his early enthusiasm and to see a little more clearly what kind of a person he was. They also show us something of what Chapel Hill must have been like in the 1820s, and how profoundly it differed from the Chapel Hill of the 1990s.

It is hard to visualize now what the country in the immediate vicinity of the University campus must have been like in the second and third decades of the nineteenth century. The University lands were still in large part forested. There were woods in all directions. Cleared fields were spotted here and there between the "Hill" and the creeks that framed it. The village in Mitchell's day hardly extended beyond Columbia Street in a westerly direction, or eastward beyond the aptly named Boundary Street. Mitchell could walk out of his house on the campus (near present-day Swain Hall) and begin finding interesting wild plants almost anywhere. We know from his notes that he went most often south, in the direction of Morgan Creek, and less often to the north and east, toward Bolin Creek. There were fish worth trapping then, at least in Morgan Creek. In Mitchell's time there were grist mills on both creeks, as well as large and active sawmills. Usually he included in his notes a few words fixing the locality of each collection (or observation) in his mind, words that powerfully evoke that rural setting, though they are often difficult to identify with modern equivalents: "on Morgan's creek a little below Kittrels fish-traps"; "from Merits meadow up to the Maples at the turn of Creek; or "through the Presidents field and down the branch." Some of his principal landmarks were "Barbee's Mill" and "Merritt's Mill" on Morgan Creek, the sawmill on Bolin ["Bollings"] Creek, and "Barbees eastern mill" on Bolin Creek. We have tried in an appendix (Appendix C) to identify Mitchell's localities as closely as possible.

The following passage, extracted from Mitchell's botanical notes,[1] illustrates some of his methods of work and provides some clues as to the credibility of his

---

[1] In the interest of readability, this and other illustrative quotations from Mitchell's journal have occasionally been altered in punctuation and spelling from the form in which they appear in our full edition, below, pp. 29–63.

identifications. His notes on individual excursions usually include, in addition to mention of the month and day, some description of where he went, and mention of one or more plants that he found — sometimes by name only, sometimes with analyses or comments, or references to the literature. It would seem from the entries in his ledger that his practice was to make tentative identifications on the spot, and then to carry home with him at least the more puzzling specimens to be studied and written up at leisure, where several different published floras were available to him as reference sources.

> April 21 [1821]. From Merits [sic] Meadow up to the Maples at the turn of Creek [Morgan Creek]. Found *Orontium aquaticum, Pedicularis canadensis, Viburnum* _____ , *Potentilla simplex* and *Arum [Arisaema] triphyllum*. A plant at the bend not ascertained. Saw also *Sysirinchium anceps* and *Hypoxis erecta*.
> *Aira [Trisetum] melicoides*. Pretty well ascertained sometime ago. Agrees with Elliotts *triflora* except that in no instance do I find three flowers or a pubescence at the bottom of the corolla.
> *Stipa avenacea*. Pursh and Elliott. There is a pretty small beard at the base of the Corolla. Tis rather hair.
> *Viola striata*. The only white violet with a stem. A good beard on the lateral petals. Procumbent agrees not with Elliott. At the Maples.
> *Viola pubescens*. Agrees with Pursh and can be no other as *hastata* is already ascertained. The lateral petals slightly bearded and the lower with streaks of purple; flowers small. Same place.
> *Chaerophyllum [Osmorhiza] claytoni*. Separated into a new genus by Nutall [sic]. *Uraspermum*. Nutalls description gives all can be desired. Same place.
> *Oxalis corniculata* about which I had some doubts [see March 29, 1820] is known by its early flowering and semi-procumbent habit.
> *Myosotis arvensis*. Which I last year [at Merritt's Meadow, April 13, 1820] called a *Lithospermum* now ascertained by comparing Pursh and Barton.
> *Arabis lyrata*. A plant common in the cultivated fields along Merits Creek having compressed siliquae I have concluded to call by this name because I can call it nothing else. Possibly right.
> *Ellisia nyctelea*. I was well satisfied about this plant before except that I could not make the loculi and seeds of the capsule agree. But I have now two valves and 3 seeds. I assume there are 4 when the plant is perfect — I found two Carexes making 4 species quite distinct I have found this year but I call no names as yet. *Ellisia* is at the corner of the fence near the Maples. (EM2, p. 147)

[In another note the next year, dated April 17, on a trip to the "bend in Morgan's Creek at the Maples," is the comment, "*Ellisia* grows plentifully by the side of a rock in the field about half a mile above this and is in flower" (p. 152).]

Mitchell identified his plants ("ascertained" them, as he said) from books. He had an excellent library for the time, eventually including most of the published floras dealing with North American plants, and it was his custom, when he attempted to identify a plant new to him, to cite the name of the author by whose work he had been able to make the decision. In notes thought to have been made in 1819, he mentioned only Bigelow, Eaton, and Elliott. The name of Pursh is absent, presumably because Mitchell did not receive a copy of Pursh's *Flora* until the winter of 1819–1820. In subsequent years it is clear from the number of times he mentioned Pursh (1816) and Elliott (1816–1824), and from his often detailed presentation of data from their respective floras, that he depended most heavily upon them. In 1820, the year during which Mitchell was most active botanically and was identifying a large number of plants new to him, he very often cited the works of one or more authors as his sources. On March 6 he said of *Sanguinaria canadensis*, "All the books." In all, he cited at least ten authorities that year, with a heavy preponderance of Elliott and Pursh. In difficult cases, he often set down in great detail the steps by which he had finally eliminated all choices except one, sometimes contrasting the work of one author with another.

Many of his plant-identifications were recorded by him in his copy of Pursh's *Flora Americae Septentrionalis* (1816), now a part of the University Library. He punctiliously underlined in that work the names of most species mentioned elsewhere in his notes on the local plants. At least three species (*Laurus caroliniensis*, *Arenaria squarrosa*, and *Liatris bellidifolia*) are underlined there with the additional note, "Wilmington [N.C.] June 20, 1823." We can suppose that he might have annotated Elliott's *Sketch* in a similar fashion as it became available to him. The first five parts of its first volume were printed in 1820, but part 6, pages 497-606, including about half of the class *Decandria* and all of class *Icosandria*, plus *Addenda*, was not published until 1821 (cf. Stafleu and Cowan, 1986); the second volume was published in seven parts between 1821 and 1824. Unfortunately, Mitchell's copy of Elliott's work is not in the University Library today.

Almost as numerous as the references to Pursh and Elliott throughout Mitchell's notes are those to "Nut[t]all" (1818) and "Rees" (1806–1818) — the last of these Mitchell also cited as "Encyclopaedia," or "(Dr.) Smith," or once "Sir E. Smith (Rees)." Less frequently, but often, he cited Barton (1815, or 1817–1818), Bigelow (1814, or 1817–1821; usually without qualification, once as "Florula Bostoniensis" and two or three times as "Med. Bot."), Eaton (1818; unqualified, or once "Eaton's Manual"), Michaux (mostly without qualification, probably chiefly in reference to the *Flora Boreali-Americana*, 1803), and Torrey (1819, or 1823–1824; once as "N.Y. Catalogue"). Some authors are mentioned a few times only, and then often as if incidentally — for example, Beck (1833; cited once in 1837), Linnaeus (cited once), and Persoon (1805–1807); or in connection with some special group of plants — for example, Bridel (1797–1818; mosses), the younger Michaux (1817–1819; "Sylva," with reference to *Quercus*), Muhlenberg (1817; grasses and sedges), Sprengel (1807; mosses; mentioned once), or Willdenow (1805, 1806; ferns, *Carex* and grasses, perhaps including some species attributed to Muhlenberg by Willdenow).

He had a copy of Catesby (1730–1732, 1737–1747), but found it disappointing ("The plates are only so-so"). He acquired Michaux's work on oaks (presumably A. Michaux, 1801) before June 1821: he was obliged, as he told Schweinitz, "to pay a pretty penny for it," but he found it a fine work "as amply to repay me the expense." By reference to the text and especially to the plates, he said, "I have ascertained with it 12 species of oak within two miles of this place to my entire satisfaction."[2] It may have been at this time that he drew up a list of the oaks

---

[2]Mitchell to Schweinitz, June 1821 (see pp. 10, 11, 52).

comparing by name those treated by Michaux with those by Elliott (EM2, p. 28).

As time went on and Mitchell became acquainted with a great many of the plants, he was inclined to record information about the plants themselves, their habitats, or their dates of flowering. He had little need to mention his sources, so smaller proportions of the years' lists are documented in this way. In 1821, by our count, he referred to eight authors — including Barton, Muhlenberg, and Torrey, none of whom had been on the list in 1820. In 1822 Mitchell's excursions were less extensive, but he cited at least seven authors, including Bridel's *Muscologia recentiorum*, whose work on mosses he had received from Schweinitz on November 8, 1821. After 1822 he made few collections and, as far as we know, few botanical observations.

Mitchell's references to the books he was using are usually brief and cryptic, set down as a way of reminding him of the means by which he had reached a certain name for a plant. Occasionally he added a comment, as "*Draba hispidula*. Pursh. Michaux. Michaux is the best by far" (EM2, p. 146), or "*Pteris aquilina*. Pursh's description is copied from Wildenow on the European Plant and is therefore good for nothing. See Bigelow who is pretty good" (p. 130). Sometimes he quoted his authors directly: "May 3d, 1837. *Phlox setacea*...calyx which in the *subulata* are a little shorter or about as long as the tube of the corolla. Torrey. Beck but in the *setacea* much shorter (Torrey) triplo brevioribus — Pursh" (p. 183). As in this quotation, and the following ones, he often compared one author with another: "*Ranunculus recurvatus*....It may be that Pursh and Dr. Smith mean different things by *lanuginosus*" (p. 147); "*Poa annua*. I had suspected from the descriptions of Elliott and Barton and the habitat as given by Elliott it was the *annua*. But Muhlenburg [*sic*] gives entire satisfaction especially characters 6.7.8.9. which leave no doubt — found in my garden" (p. 148).

Because these references to books cite an author's name only, and rarely the title of the work itself, it is not always possible to be sure which work of a certain author Mitchell was citing. There is no problem with authors such as Pursh and Elliott, who each wrote but a single work that would be relevant. For authors like Amos Eaton, whose *Manual* went through four editions between 1817 and 1824, we have tried to include in our bibliography the edition that Mitchell most probably would have found available about 1820–1823. For authors like W. P. C. Barton and Jacob Bigelow, who each wrote both a flora and a work on medical botany, it is usually impossible to be sure which is intended. Those few works still in the library that are stamped **E. Mitchell** or **University Library, N.C.**, date from Mitchell's period and so could have been used by him (see M. R. McVaugh, 1987). When Michaux is cited, probably the *Flora boreali-americana* of André Michaux is usually meant, but both his *Chênes* (1801) and the *Sylva* of François-André Michaux (1817–1819) seem also to have been available to Mitchell.

Artificial keys for the identification of genera and species, commonplace in the twentieth century, were little used in Mitchell's time, and were not found in the books that he used, except that most floras were so arranged that the text itself provided a number of critical separations. The Linnaean sexual system of classification, though nearing the end of its active life, was still used in almost all floras published up to about 1820, including the works of Pursh and Elliott, Mitchell's principal sources. To find an unknown, one worked tediously and systematically through the major divisions, and finally hoped to reach a conclusion by comparing a number of descriptions of genera, eliminating one possibility after another, often after consulting several different authorities. To find an unknown plant in Pursh's *Flora*, for example, it was necessary first to know the number of stamens in the flower (the primary division under the Linnaean system), then the number of pistils, then to select from a list of briefly characterized genera in the chosen category. To our eyes these groups of genera seem strange: there is no separation by plant-families as we know them, and even both monocots and dicots may be found in the same small group. With time and patience, however, it was often possible to arrive at a reasonable identification, because the brief characterizations, in the Linnaean manner, constituted a key of sorts. Once arrived at the name of the genus, a similar procedure was carried out to determine the name of the species. Linnaeus and those who used his system held that by using a description (the Linnaean "character" that differed for each species) of not more than twelve carefully chosen contrasting words, it was possible to distinguish a species from all other members of its genus. For small genera this worked well enough, but it was not very useful for an area (like the North Carolina of 1820) in which there were to be found additional genera (or species) unknown to the author of the flora, taxa that could be distinguished only by longer descriptions.

Mitchell's notes provide us with what must be almost a unique contemporary account from the period before dichotomous keys were common, of the steps that had to be followed in order to identify an unknown species of plant from the floras that were available at the time. If the plant belonged to a genus with many species, it was necessary first to eliminate species after species by referring to the published descriptions, and often by comparing the descriptions of the same species in different floras, until one arrived at a small group of species or, if one was fortunate, at one single species that could not be eliminated. It was Mitchell's practice to keep notes on species as he eliminated each one, citing the serial numbers under which they had been arranged in the floras he was using. Some of the best examples of how he worked are presented in full below. His attempts at identification met with varying degrees of success, as judged on the basis of modern knowledge.

(1) In some instances his approach (perhaps through no fault of his own) led him to a conclusion that, in light of what we know now, does not seem to be the correct one. These may be illustrated by his treatments of an unknown *Ranunculus*, and of what he called *Ellisia*, *Arabis*, and *Chaerophyllum*.

In April of (probably) 1825, he returned to study a species of *Ranunculus* that he had called *R. fascicularis* in 1820. Working with plants from approximately the same locality, he wrote down a detailed description of what he saw, then proceeded:

> Not abortivus or nitidus of Pursh because I know the abortivus. Not sceleratus fide Elliott and Encyclopaedia on account of the nectary and great number of stamens. Not 10. of Pursh from its habitat — nor 12 from its fibrous root. Not 19 from its small flower nor 22. 23. There remains — /Encyclopaedia/ — 9.11.13.14.15.16.17.18.21./22.46.51.54.59.63.65.66.68.69/ . Not 9 fide Encyclopaedia on account of the scale. Not 11. fide Encyclopaedia on account of the large petals and shaggy calyx. Not 13. fide Ency. aut hirsutus because it has no tubercles. Not 14. from the want of runners and of an obcordate scale Ency. Not 15. which I shall see in flower late in June next. Fide Bigelow Med. Bot. Not 16 from the large heart shaped

quinquefid leaves and striated flower stalks of 16. Not 17. Fide Encyclop. Not 18 which has a smooth calyx. Not 20 from the globular fruit of 20. and its almost smooth calyx otherwise it agrees pretty well. Not 21 from the small pale yellow flowers of 21.

I have formerly called it the fascicularis and now believe I am right and that it is likewise the nitidus of Elliott which is rendered *very* probable by the *square scale* and *many filaments*. See Eaton's Manual and Florula Bostoniensis. (EM2, p. 186)

The method did not always bring one to the correct answer (which of course applies also to the now universal dichotomous key). According to Radford *et al.* (1968), *Ranunculus fascicularis* does not occur in North Carolina. In that species the fascicled roots are very thick and fleshy, which Mitchell could hardly have failed to notice. His description suggests *R. hispidus* Michx., a low spring-flowering plant common around Chapel Hill.

Sometimes Mitchell found the right answer in the book, but he was wrong because the real answer was unknown to Pursh, and Pursh's description was not detailed enough to be helpful. His account of plants found in the valley of Morgan Creek (above, p. 19) illustrates this nicely. Take, for example, his report of *Ellisia nyctelea*. Pursh had included *Ellisia nyctelea* in his *Flora*, with the statement that it had been found in Virginia "on the banks of the Potowmac" (1816, p. 141). The range-extension to North Carolina must have seemed a reasonable one to Mitchell. Using Pursh's summary of the genera in the Linnaean division called *Pentandria Monogynia*, Mitchell must have searched (as his report suggests) among the eight genera listed as having a bilocular capsule. Perhaps eliminating genera that he already knew, like *Datura* with deciduous calyx, and *Verbascum* with bearded filaments, and having seen Pursh's statement "Flowers white, very small," he settled on *Ellisia*. Almost certainly his plant was not *Ellisia*, which is scarcely known to occur anywhere south of the Potomac and east of the Mississippi. It is very probable that what he found was a closely related but distinctively different plant that does grow in the Southeast, but was unknown to Pursh: namely, *Nemophila aphylla*, not found in modern times in Orange County, but often collected in alluvial soils in stream valleys in neighboring counties only a few miles from Mitchell's locality. His erroneous identification of the plant as *Ellisia* was perpetuated by M. A. Curtis's report of it as a North Carolina plant (Curtis, 1867, p. 42).

A comparable instance is that of *Arabis lyrata*, also reported from Morgan Creek, about whose identity Mitchell was somewhat doubtful. The species is of more northerly range, known from the mountains of North Carolina but not from the Piedmont. It is unlikely that he found it in Chapel Hill. He may have known it in New England, however, and the plant that reminded him of it in Chapel Hill, because of its pinnately dissected basal leaves, was most probably what is now called *Sibara virginica*, a common field weed in the Piedmont of North Carolina. Pursh knew it as *Cardamine virginica*. Mitchell apparently decided that it was an *Arabis*, because of the compressed siliques that he mentioned, and that brought him to *A. lyrata*, one of the two species of *Arabis* listed by Pursh, and the only one reported from the United States.

Mitchell also reported *Chaerophyllum* [= *Osmorhiza*] *claytoni* from the Morgan Creek valley. As known to Pursh and to Elliott, the genus *Chaerophyllum* included no more than three species in the Southeast. Once arrived at the genus, Mitchell's obvious choice was *C. claytoni*, a plant originally described by Michaux from Carolina. This, like *Arabis lyrata*, is primarily a mountain species in North Carolina. The plant of the Piedmont, presumably the one that Mitchell saw, is *Osmorhiza longistylis*, a species not known to science until 1824 and therefore not listed by Pursh or Elliott.

Because of such difficulties with existing reference works, and perhaps even more because Mitchell had no named series of specimens against which to compare what he found in the vicinity of Chapel Hill, there was necessarily a degree of uncertainty in all his identifications of unknowns, especially in the larger or more difficult genera. Even today, with modern illustrated descriptive floras, critical determinations are often impossible without direct comparison with another specimen that has been authenticated by a specialist. When Mitchell had little or no prior knowledge of a group, and the descriptions in existing floras were scanty and subjective, the names at which he arrived were sometimes, as he said, "mere guesses."

In less difficult genera his identifications were apparently dependable, though it is impossible to be sure, because we have no herbarium specimens from him. Although we cannot vouch for all of his identifications, there is often no reason to question them. When he reported such things as *Hepatica triloba, Erythronium americanum, Stellaria pubera, Saxifraga virginiensis, Epigaea repens, Sanguinaria canadensis, Dentaria heterophylla, Anemone thalictroides,* and *Claytonia virginica* flowering on wooded hillsides near the creeks, between February 27 and March 12, there can be little doubt what he had (though the names may have been changed), as these are the common spring flowers in that habitat. He mentioned in all between 350 and 400 different species that he had "ascertained," growing near Chapel Hill. About 85% of these, under the same or different names, are identifiable today with some confidence, and still grow in Orange County or have been found there in the past (data from Radford et al., 1968).

(2) Sometimes Mitchell's notes made it clear that his identification was the correct one, as two examples will attest:

> March 24, [1820]. *Asarum virginicum*. I think I found this in full flower on the N. side of the Hill. It is distinguished from the *arifolium* which is common on the S side of the Hill by the shape of the leaf [and] its colour. This [*virginicum*] being lighter with veins of white — that [*arifolium*] is purplish — by flowering earlier — the *arifolium* is not yet in flower and by the different taste of the root — that of the ["*virginicum*" crossed out] *arifolium* much resembling *Sassafras*.
>
> *Asarum arifolium*. Common. The flowers much longer than the *virginicum* [—] *coarctatum* — and without the deep purple colour in the inside. (EM2, p. 114)

These two species, now often treated as species of the genus *Hexastylis*, still flourish in upland woods around Chapel Hill, separated exactly as indicated by Mitchell. One, *H. minor*, sometimes flowers a month ahead of the other. The word *coarctatum* in the quotation above is from Pursh, evidently Mitchell's authority, who said of *A. arifolium*: "calyce tuboloso infra limbum...coarctato" (1816, p. 597).

Another example of how Mitchell worked and reasoned correctly is the following:

> May 1st [1820]. From Merits down the creek on the other side to the Whetstone Rocks.
> *Rhododendron punctatum*. I am utterly unable to decide whether it be not *maximum roseum*. The very short calix and red corolla seem to be decisive, yet the long pedicells and leaves whitish on the under side are opposed. On the whole I think I am right. The habitat of *punctatum* however seems to be in the mountains on the heads of the great rivers. The same plant I now have grows on the Pilot Mountain. (EM2, p. 122)

Mitchell was evidently following Pursh, who described *punctatum* as having pink-red flowers and "dentibus calycis brevissimis" (p. 298). His identification was correct; he had the plant now commonly called *Rhododendron catawbiense*.

(3) In addition to the rather large number of Mitchell's reports that can be taken on faith, and the smaller number of doubtful and unidentifiable records, there remains a residue of names that are of interest because they may (if correctly reported) represent valid records of species that are no longer known from Orange County, or have never been reported from there except by Mitchell. Several such are still common or well known in sandy open meadows or open acid boggy places in the Coastal Plain of North Carolina, but scarcely known outside that province. These habitats, probably never very common in the Piedmont, have now become rare there because of intensive agricultural use of the land accompanied by clearing and draining. It is reasonable to suppose that some plants, nearly or quite restricted to such habitats, at one time ranged locally into the lower Piedmont.

A prime example of such a species is *Orontium aquaticum*, a conspicuous spring-flowering aroid that was mentioned by Mitchell on April 21, 1821, and on other occasions, as growing in pools and low places near Morgan Creek. The plant is unmistakable when in flower, and was well described by both Pursh and Elliott. In North Carolina it is common in the Coastal Plain and scattered elsewhere, least common in the Piedmont and not otherwise reported from Orange County although known from adjoining Alamance and Chatham Counties. There seems little reason to doubt Mitchell's report.

An even more intriguing mention of a Coastal Plain species is Mitchell's entry for March 10, [1820], as follows: "March 10. Laurus diospyrus. Pursh. Nutall. Good. Dioicous? Nutall. Found in the Pond S.E. from College. Dried the blossoms" (EM2, p. 113). A second mention of the plant appears two years later: "Feby. 22, [1822]. Down about Scotts hole — ascertained the shrub in the pond to be Laurus geniculata of Pursh and Elliott" (EM2, p. 151). It is difficult to believe that Mitchell, acute as he was, could have reached the determination he did unless he really had the plant in question, or something very like it. In the Linnaean system used by both Pursh and Elliott the group *Enneandria* (having nine stamens) was a very small one including but three genera, two of which were herbaceous and the other, *Laurus*, was woody. The latter included what are now called *Sassafras albidum* and *Lindera benzoin*, both of which were known to Mitchell as species of *Laurus*. The flowers are so unusual that he would hardly have assigned another species to the same genus unless the flowers corresponded. If "Laurus geniculata" had been a common plant of Orange County the identification would not have been questioned. As it is, the so-called Pond Spice or Pondberry, now officially called *Lindera melissifolia*, is a rare shrub, known today in North Carolina from but three populations in two counties in the southeastern part of the Coastal Plain.³ Until the actual specimens collected by Mitchell were found recently in the herbarium of the Academy of Natural Sciences of Philadelphia (see above, p. 11), it seemed unlikely that it had ever occurred in ponds in the lower Piedmont, where natural ponds are rare. Evidently Scott's Hole was such a pond in Mitchell's time. Its name was current in botanical circles in Chapel Hill at least into the second decade of this century, but seems now to have been forgotten. If it has escaped the blight of urban development, Mitchell's plant may eventually be rediscovered there. The plant was reported from North Carolina by M. A. Curtis (1860, 1867), on Mitchell's authority, under the name of *Benzoin melissaefolium*. It would be interesting to know if Curtis saw a specimen collected by Mitchell, or merely accepted a report without verifying it.

(4) Even after Mitchell was devoting most of his time to geology and other matters, he made efforts from time to time to "get acquainted," as he said, with such difficult groups in the local flora as *Panicum*, *Poa*, *Carex*, *Quercus*, *Hedysarum* [*Desmodium*], *Aster*, and *Solidago*. Except for the oaks (a list derived from the works of Michaux and Elliott), he was seldom confident about the results of his studies, most of which he did not pursue in depth. The undated study headed "The genus Aster" (EM2, pp. 180–181) is a list of seven binomials and four species designated merely as *Aster*, including a short description (based on Pursh), and with notes like "on a rock near Hillsborough" or "with a very large flower." Also undated, but apparently contemporary with *Aster*, "The genus Solidago" (pp. 182–183) lists *S. bicolor*, *S. aspera*, and *S. odora* by name only, and five unnamed species briefly characterized as "the one in the grove," "the tallest," "of a gray colour." Apparently a little more time was spent on a list of "paniculate Panica," including seven named and two unnamed species (pp. 178–179).

Sometimes Mitchell's method, no matter how carefully followed, led him to frustration. This was particularly true with respect to the genus *Carex*, where identifications right or wrong were hard for him to achieve. He probably devoted more study to *Carex* than to any other genus, as suggested by the amount of space devoted to it in his notes. Sometimes he worried about a single knotty point for years, and made detailed observations and extensive notes; the first note below was dated May 6, 1822:

Carex festucacea. The plant I have must of course lie between Nos. 15 and 22 inclusive [i.e., the species so numbered in Pursh's flora]. The number of spiculae which in 16 specimens are on 9—5, on 5—6 and on 2—8, excludes at once Nos. 15, 16, 19, and the want of "bracteae foliaceae longissimae" excludes No. 21. There remains Nos. 17, 18, 20, 22. Nos. 18 [and] 20 are at first to be suspected — from the numbers of Spiculae "Spiculis subsenis" 2. from the habitat "New York." 20 is thrown out by Muhlenburg [sic] who describes it as having only the terminal spicules

---

³It is a plant always found growing in ponds, or seasonally flooded wetlands, formerly widely distributed in such habitats in the Coastal Plain from Arkansas to North Carolina, but now greatly reduced in numbers and officially listed as an endangered species. The U.S. Fish and Wildlife Service, Atlanta, Ga., in 1993 offered a "Recovery Plan for Pondberry (*Lindera melissifolia* [Walt.] Blume)" by Linda DeLay, Roslyn O'Conner, Joe Ryan, and Robert R. Currie (56 unnumbered pages, processed); this report listed 36 naturally occurring populations, 23 of which are in Arkansas or Mississippi.

"basi Mascula" also Caps ovata *integra*. *Festucacea* agrees pretty well with Pursh. It does not agree well with Muhlenburg. Description 10 to 18 inches high when in seed; culm has two or three leaves, linear, extending to the height of 5 or 6 inches; the rest is bare — nearly round — striate where the leaves cease — becoming triquetrous at top. Spiculae alternate clavate obtuse. Female scale lanceolate membranous with a green keel about tho hardly as long as the capsule, mucronate. Capsule lenticular bicuspidate ciliate serrate especially near the apex. In my garden. April. I think I have the *Festucacea* at least of Pursh. (EM2, p. 111)

Evidently never wholly satisfied with this, Mitchell returned in 1828 to what he took to be the same plant, consulting this time not only Pursh (1816) and Muhlenberg's *Descriptio uberior graminum* (1817), but Barton (1820–1824), and J. E. Smith's treatment of *Carex* in Rees's *Cyclopaedia*. As we remarked above, he seems to have been unaware of Schweinitz's monographic papers on *Carex* (1824, 1825).

An old enemy. Grows in wet ground at least generally. Stigmas two — spikes androgynous — masculine at the base. In the class between 15 and 22 of Pursh. 8. to which is to be added *Straminea* from Barton and Encyclopaedia. No. 17 [and] 21 are thrown out [by] "Bracteis foliaceis longissimis," No. 15 [by] "Spiculis tribus congestis" of Pursh and Ency. No. 16 by P and Muhlenburg "Foliis glaucis scabris — Spicis tribus — infima bracteata ceteris ebracteatis — Bractea spicula longiore" together with the remark. No. 18 by Smith "Culmus acute triqueter." "Bractea foliacea ad basin spiculae infimae" "Flores masculi pauci foeminei numerosae." —— *Straminea*. "Spike compound —— *Spikelets* subglobose almost close together." Barton. Muhlenburg.

Improbable — No. 22 "Spikelets about 8, merely close together" — Barton — fruit larger than the scale. Yet it may be *scoparia*, *festucacea*, *curta* with which last *canescens*, *elongata* and *loliacea* are said to be the same. Ency. Descriptions Culm 10 to 18 inches. *Obscurely triquetrous* except toward the top — striate. Rough at the edges within 3 inches of the top. leafy from 1/3 to 1/2 its height. Leaves linear carinate rough at the edges only, not as long as the culms ligula membranaceous. Spikes 6, sometimes 5 or 7 — seldom 4 or 8, cylindrical, masculine below, the male part at first occupying two thirds of the spike — the spikes near yet perfectly distinct. A membranaceous, green, carinate awned bractea always appearing, 1/2 as long including the awn as the spike in the lowest, diminishing so as almost to disappear above, perhaps withering and deciduous, not pubescent but very smooth. Scale ovate membranaceous green, carinate, acute. Stamina 3, white. Capsule notandum. Against the three species between which it lies are the following characters. Muhlen.

Festucacea. Spike composite — Spikelets 8. — Caps.

Curta. *Lower* spike with linear pubescent bractea, and the *terminal* masculine at the base. Caps. is if recollect right a good deal toothed

Scoparia. Spike composite. Spikelets 5, the lowest bracteated. Caps.

As Willdenow gives to *Scoparia* a lanceolate mucronate bractea, a marginate capsule, I shall call it at present *Carex scoparia*. [This last sentence was crossed out and the following words added: "Is it not *brizoides*? cf Cyclopaedia."] (EM2, pp. 107–108)

One can feel Mitchell's frustration. He was laboring under a great disadvantage. In the southeastern United States, according to Small (1933), there are no fewer than 130 species of *Carex*. In 1816 Pursh knew only 64 species in all North America, which for all practical purposes meant the northeastern states and adjacent Canada. There was about a fifty-fifty chance that when Mitchell worked on a *Carex*, he spent all his time and effort on running down a species that was not in the books he used. According to Radford et al. (1968), 44 species of *Carex* have been reported from Orange County. A list of local species compiled by Mitchell, probably in April 1828 (EM2, pp.100-108), included species numbered 1–21, with detailed analyses of five, and localities mentioned for eight or nine more. No. 13 was omitted from the list, and three were unnamed. The "old enemy," that problem species, is between 20 and 21.

MITCHELL'S BOTANICAL NOTES

Mitchell began occasional botanical explorations of Chapel Hill and its vicinity in 1819, and during the season of 1820 he made botanical observations every few days from early spring at least to September. He seems to have followed much the same pattern in the next few years until new responsibilities led him away from botany. In a letter to Schweinitz (June 1821) he wrote: "I have not determined what to do with myself during the vacation. It is at any rate to be given to botany." We are necessarily a little vague, however, about the exact dates of his wanderings because of the way he kept his notes. He seems not to have kept a regular daybook. Instead, he entered his notes and comments on botany in a large ledger (Elisha Mitchell Papers, MS vol. 2; Southern Historical Collection, University of North Carolina Library) that he had previously partially filled with charts, tables, and notes on other subjects that had interested him from time to time. His records of individual excursions, which usually included a mention of month and day (but unfortunately in most instances not the year), occupy not only new pages, but also vacant spaces in partially filled pages. For example, a half-page devoted to the history of astronomy, and notes on mosses dated March 9, 1822, are sandwiched in among nine pages devoted to an enumeration of 21 species of *Carex*, some parts of which are dated April 1828. The second page of a long discussion on the history and theory of electricity ends near the top of the page, and is closely followed, separated only by an inked line, by botanical notes beginning February 21, 1823.

Most of the pages numbered 12, 16–19, 28, 100–153, 178–189, and 207 are devoted to botany, but in no discernible order. A note on p. 18, "Engaged once more in Botany," is dated September 19, 1835; a note on p. 207 is dated February 5, 1821; notes from October 1821 are on p. 184; on p. 186, with the heading, "I now take up my botanical studies for the first time this year," the date is clearly written April 5, 1815 (the date perhaps an error for 1825, as the note mentions several books published after 1815); and on p. 188, under "More Botany," are entries for Christmas Day, 1824, and, immediately following, May 3, 1837.

Concentrated between pages 112 and 153 of Mitchell's ledger book, there is a long series of what appear to be consecutive entries, chronologically arranged, beginning in February 1820 and ending (after some interruptions) in April 1823, a period corresponding to that of his most intensive botanical work. It is rarely possible to be sure of the year of any particular excursion, because Mitchell rarely made a note of it, and there are some dated entries from later years mixed into the series of 1820–1823. We know from Mitchell's correspondence with Schweinitz that because of the need for more books he was not botanizing very actively in 1819, but it seems certain that his day-by-day notes on his excursions began in 1820.

We give below a transcription of those entries recording Mitchell's botanizing in the Chapel Hill of 1819–1823, together with some infrequent notes from as late as 1837. In the earliest long series of entries, from 1820, the species are numbered by Mitchell in order from 1 to 67 (up to *Hieracium venosum*, Apr. 17); we have not included these numbers. We have rearranged the entries into chronological sequence; numbers in square brackets refer to the pagination of Mitchell's ledger, and an exclamation point following a date [!] emphasizes that the year can be established from Mitchell's notes. Many of the notes are interlined, and the interlineations have been indicated /in this manner/. Except for his abbreviations for the months, which we have standardized in the interest of easier reference, we have not altered his spelling. We may note, with respect to his reference works, that Mitchell almost invariably spells "Nuttall" as "Nutall," "Muhlenberg" as "Muhlenburg,"and usually refers to Rees's *Cyclopaedia* as "Encyclopaedia." Localities referred to personal names have been identified as far as possible and are listed in Appendix C.

At the beginning of this project, our goal was to provide an exact transcription of the botanical notes, but we soon found that this was impractical because of Mitchell's idiosyncratic and often telegraphic prose, and especially because of his practices in capitalization and puctuation. We have therefore made a certain number of arbitrary decisions in transcribing. Mitchell often inconsistently capitalized words that are not capitalized in the same context today (and vice versa). We have removed much of his capitalization; specifically, we have decapitalized all specific epithets in accordance with modern taxonomic usage. Latin names of plants have been italicized in our commentary, but in Mitchell's text they have been set in ordinary (Roman) type. Mitchell occasionally used underlining to emphasize words or phrases in the text, and we have preserved this emphasis by the use of italic, but we have chosen not to underline his plant-names (as if for italic in the modern editorial convention), as he almost invariably did not do so himself. Individual dates have been set in **boldface,** for easy reference.

Punctuation presented us with special problems. Mitchell seems to have had his own rules, but he was not consistent in applying them. In ordinary narrative prose he commonly used short sentences ending with a period. Sometimes, however, he omitted the terminal period entirely, or replaced it by a horizontal line like a short or long dash. Many of his notes summarize the steps he went through in identifying a particular plant, and in these summaries his style became noticeably more telegraphic, including few verbs, many periods in what seem to us unnecessary places, periods in series where we would normally expect semicolons or colons, or periods in addition to dashes as mentioned above. For what appears to have seemed to him a change of thought, or perhaps merely for emphasis, he would insert a dash both before and after a word or words in a sentence. Frequently, after making a tentative identification, he revised his opinion after consulting his authorities, or merely after fuller consideration. Such revised opinions often appear in the notes, in the form of interlinear additions, replacements of crossed-out words, or supplementary sentences or phrases crowded into spaces that happened to have been left vacant. The notes were evidently not written so as to be clear to other readers but to serve as reminders to Mitchell himself, as a lecturer may set down key words to remind himself of whole subjects.

The result of this telegraphic style, combined with Mitchell's habits of (apparently randomly) inserting or leaving out punctuation marks at unexpected places, or inserting what seem to us to be irrelevant or perhaps even unintended marks, is to obscure his meaning in some places in the longer or more complicated expositions. It is usually possible, by following his notes step by step in conjunction with the relevant source (flora) to make his conclusion understandable (and very commonly plausible); but not always. In our opinion, faithful transcriptions of such paragraphs, *verbatim et literatim*, tend to obfuscate the passage for even the most assiduous and botanically well informed reader. Somewhat reluctantly, therefore, we have elected to edit Mitchell's punctuation, for the sake of clarification. Where it has been omitted, we have added a period after species-names that introduce a paragraph. We have deleted what seem to be irrelevant or misleading marks (like the period Mitchell almost always placed after the words "Not" and "Nor"). We have closed parentheses and quotations when Mitchell failed to do so. We have treated Mitchell's expansible horizontal lines as if they were uniformly en-dashes, and have omitted them where they seemed to serve no purpose, as at the ends of lines. But we have tried to keep our changes to a minimum, and the resulting transcription still, we believe, retains the flavor of the amateur naturalist at work.

1819 [?]

[112] Botanical Studies

May 15. Salvia lyrata ascertained. Elliott p. 31. Description good ex. 1–2 feet high. tube of corolla 3 times as long as the calyx. Lyre Too[thed] Sage. Cancer Weed.

Tradescantia virginica ascertained. Elliott p. 280 [actually 380]. Des. good. Quaerenda. Root creeping. Stem branching, leaves ciliate, Flower heads divided into rows. Found one locality N of Mr. Kitterells on the high grounds between the fields.

Antirrhinum canadense. Compare Bigelow and Eaton. Description good. Corolla bilabiate. Upper lip reflex. 2 lobed. lower spreading 3.cleft. Between my house and college.

Sep 16. Lobelia amoena. Determined.

[The above is undated as to year. It immediately precedes the following entries for 1820. Pursh, a flora that was not available to Mitchell until 1820, but was used and quoted assiduously then and afterward, is not cited. The formal title of "Botanical Studies," the citations of pages from Elliott, and vernacular names of the *Salvia* from the same source, apparently reflect a system of notation initiated by Mitchell at the beginning of his botanical excursions but not continued in later years. As he wrote to Schweinitz later in the summer of 1819, his botanical studies that year were not extensive because of his lack of books. For all these reasons, and because of their position in the ledger, we presume that the few notes above constitute most of those made in 1819.]

1820

Feb 25. Narcissus pseudo-narcissus. Common Daffodil. Determined Sec. Rees. Cyclopaedia (Article) Narcissus.

Prunus chicasa.– Pursh. Correct "gemmis aggregatis bifloris" *g.a.trifloris* "April. May." *Feb. March C. Hill.*

Laurus benzoin. Pursh. Description good but the best account of the genus is in Nutall.

Vaccinium corymbosum. Pursh and Bigelow. In the swamp west of woods. Found it also in great quantities N.E. from the Hill near the creek on the south side. West of Mr. Lewis's.

Feb 27. Hepatica triloba. Pursh. Good. Common. Dried. In great quantities on the bank of the same creek in moist ground.

Mar 1. Erythronium americanum (lanceolatum Pursh). Nutall. Description good with exceptions. "The three interior petals usually furnished with a callous." "dentures on each side near the base and a nectariferous pore" *Which I have never been able to find* "Leaves thickly covered with superficial punctures"? "Stigma entire" *Stigma trifid*. On the southern bank of the same creek in shady places.

Viola cucullata. Elliott Pursh Nutall Bigelow. Good. Provided the natural situation of the flower be with the single petals uppermost? Along the same creek.

Stellaria pubera. Nutall. /Rather media from a lack of ciliae/ Not so woolly as I expected to find it nor as much
[113]   ciliate in the leaves. It cannot however be the S. media because there the leaves have petioles and in these specimens they are sessile. Nor are the flowers as large as I expected to find them. Query. Is not both this and the pubera of Michaux Pursh and Nutall the S. dichotoma of Linn. Found only one specimen (March 2d) on the same creek. Dried.

[Mitchell recast the notes he took on these days and assembled them in a briefer calendar, one which we insert here:]

[141]   Calendar of Flora

Feb 25. A few flowers of Amygdalus persica fully expanded within 24 hours. Some branches of some shrubs of Prunus chicasa also in full bloom within about the same time.

Feb 26. Found Laurus benzoin in full bloom and some blossoms of Vaccinium corymbosum open.

Feb 27. Laurus sassafras in bloom in a few instances.

Feb 28. Hepatica triloba in flower.

Mar 1. Erythronium americanum in full flower. Viola cucullata opening.

Mar 2. Stellaria pubera in flower. Weather cold since last nigh[t] and that kind of cloud in the sky which brings snow squalls in N. England.

Mar 3. Peach blossoms most of which were fully expanded probably killed by the severe cold of last night. Weather still cold.

[113]   **Mar 4.** Saxifraga virginiensis (vernalis Bigelow) Description good. Pursh and Bigelow. Found on the bank of the creek between Barby's and Merits Mills. North side near where a small branch runs down a ravine into it.

Epigaea repens. Same creek the other side a little above. Pursh. Nutall. Bigelow. Encyclopaedia. Descriptions good. That in the Encyclopaedia wants correcting. "Calix double the outer consisting of 3 ovato-lanceolate pointed leaves of which the external one is larger than the rest." *Is smaller than the rest*. "Filaments 10 threadshaped the length of the tube" *I think my specimens must have been imperfect as I found only rudiments of stamens around the capsule*. Dried.

Cardamine virginica. Pursh. Good. Not very distinct from pennsylvaniana which is the only species with which there is any danger of confounding it and I some think that the virginica of Pursh is the pennsylvaniana of Wildenow. Dried. To be further examined. [Then, in smaller lettering:] – Correct. Tis lobed auricalte [?auriculate]. Per. is dentate.

Mar 6. Sanguinaria canadensis. All the books. Good. Dried. Found a little below Mr Kittrells spring.

Dentaria heterophylla. Found first above the crossing place below Kittrells on the other side March 25. below Merits on this side. Agrees with heterophylla except in 4 particulars. The whole plant very smooth – no where ciliate – leaflets never an inch long. Flowers March. Flowers white with a light tinge of rose colour. Not tenella. Leaves not sessile. Not [illegible]-elliptic. Petals not cuneate. flowers not purple.

Mar 9. Anemone thalictroides. Common. *Bigelow* Pursh good. Dried. All the specimens which I found were 3-flowered but I think they were small.

Mar 10. Laurus diospyrus. Pursh Nutall. Good. Dioicous? Nutall. Found in the pond S.E. from College. Dried the blossoms.

Mar 12. Claytonia virginica. Elliott. Good. Near Bowlings Creek W.N.W. of village.

Mar 13. Pyrus botryapium. Shad Flower of the N. States. Eaton. Pursh. Have seen only the flowers. Leaves and fruit to be examined though I have no doubt. One locality on Bolling's creek in Mr. Taylors field. Aronia ["Pursh" crossed out] Nutall Persoon.

[114]   **Mar 13.** Viola bicolor Nutall. arvensis Elliott. "Stem simple" *Branched*. The rest perfect in Nutall. Dried. By the side of the near road to Hillsborough North of the village in the descent of the hill.

Mar 16. Cercis canadensis. One bud expanded (Red Bud). Not to be mistaken. Foliage to be examined.

Orontium aquaticum (Golden Club). No doubt. In the pond near the creek below Mr Kittrells. To be further examined.

Mar 24. Asarum virginicum. I think I found this in full flower on the N. side of the Hill. It is distinguished from the arifolium which is common on the S side of the Hill by the shape of the leaf – its colour. This being lighter with veins of white – that is purplish – by flowering earlier – the arifolium is not yet in flower and by the different taste of the root – that of the ["virginicum" crossed out] arifolium much resembling Sassafras.

Asarum arifolium. Common. The flowers much longer than the virginicum [–] coarctatum – and without the deep purple colour in the inside.

Veronica peregrina. Pursh is meagre. Elliott is good except that the plant is not so large as one would expect from him. Perhaps it will continue to flower and grow larger. Account in the Encyclopaedia very good – also that of the genus. Very common. generally very small erect resembles Penstam. [?*Penstemon*].

Spergula saginoides. Pursh. Brief. Smaller than I expected perhaps owing to the soil. Description good however. See Encyclopaedia also. Peduncles not quite long enough. But little doubt. In the lot west of the house.

Podophyllum peltatum. Pursh. Nutall. Bigelow. Encyclopaedia. Common.
Phlox subulata (Wild Pink). Elliott. Pursh. Compared. Can be confounded only with aristata from which however it is sufficiently distinct.
Viola palmata dilatata. Elliott. A good account of the violet most common about C. Hill in the beginning of April. "The exteriour division dilated and toothed" to be particularly remarked. Only two opposite petals bearded.

Mar 28. See Pursh [these two words perhaps intended to follow the preceding item].

Viburnum prunifolium. Leaves to be hereafter examined.

[115]   **Mar 29.** Zanthorriza apiifolia. On Morgan's creek a little below Kittrels fish traps. No doubt.– though to be farther examined with respect to the styles. Pursh. Elliott. Nutall.

Oxalis corniculata. Common. Not lyoni because the peduncles are not two flowered. Corniculata from the procumbent stem & cuneate petals.

Gnaphalium plantagineum. Pursh and Bigelow. There can be no doubt. See Pursh. I wish there were also an account of the female flower. Tis coloured.

Mar 30. Callitriche heterophylla. Pursh. Elliott. In the ditch along the upper part of Merits Meadow. Found spathulate but not linear emarginate leaves. Perhaps from the bad state of this plant from standing in water.

Arabis thaliana. Pursh. Encyclopaedia. From the description time and place of flowering there can be little or no doubt.

Amaryllis atamasco. Elliott. To be read over again.

Gelseminum nitidum. (Yellow Jessamine). In flower in Mrs. Hoopers garden. Found in abundance between Merit and Barbees Mills. Pursh. Elliott places it in the order Monoginia. To be examined.

Lathyrus venosus. Pursh alone who had seen only specimens and I am therefore inclined to think I have the plant though somewhat different. The leaves are illiptical and the peduncles 10–30 flowered. Along the hill side in the upper end of Merits Meadow.

Apr 1. Ranunculus abortivus. Pursh. Description very good. Found by the side of the ditch in Merits Meadow.

Anemone nemorosa. Pursh. Bigelow. Can be confounded only with lancifolia from which it is distinguished by its *cuneate* inciso-lobate leaves. Found specimens above Kittrells crossing place on the other side.

Oxalis violacea. Pursh. Determined by the colour of its petals. Common.

Staphylea trifolia. Pursh. Above Kittrells fish traps on the other side. Leaves to be further examined.

Apr 5. Smyrnium cordatum of Elliott, Encyclopaedia and ["Nuttall" crossed out]. No doubt. Trifoliatum of Nutall. Determined only by the leaves. Fruit to be examined. Flowers yellow. See ["Pursh" crossed out] Nutall. Found the 3 leaved unilateral involucele.

[116]   Smyrnium aureum. I am not so clear respecting this, though there can be no great doubt from the appearance and time of flowering of the plant. Has /has an unilateral two leaved/ the same unilateral three leaved involucele with the last. Varies a good deal I believe in its foliage according to the soil in which it grows. Sometimes simply ternate – twice ternate – twice ternate with the middle lobe again divided into three – thrice ternate – thrice ternate with the middle leaf as before. Common like the last in warm dry soils – Root and seed to be examined. See Elliott and Encyclopaedia.

Pyrus melanocarpa (aronia of Persoon and Nutall). Pursh. distinguished from ovalis by the smooth calyx and from alnifolia of Nutall by the cymose corymb and the serrature extending throughout the leaf. East of College in wet ground one locality. Fruit and leaves to be again examined.

Euphorbia [blank]. A new species? On the hill side above Kittrells fish traps.

Pedicularis canadensis. Pedicularis from the mucronate capsule, canadensis from the yellowish white ["calyx" crossed out] setaceous corolla, truncated calyx and stalk leafy and woolly below the head. Pursh. Bigelow. Above the f[ish] traps this side.

Vaccinium tenellum. Pursh. From its green branches – red corolla, green calyx and mucronate and oval leaves.– I see none yet that are serrulate. N.B. tis corymbose. I have seen it serrulate.

Apr 6. Lamium amplexicaule. Encyclopaedia. Mr. Taylor's field below the Prep. Schoolhouse.

Dalibarda [= *Waldsteinia*] fragaroides. I have found no flower with more than 5 ["stamens" crossed out] styles. In the same field on the lately cleared side hill. Determined a good deal by the leaves &c yet I have very little doubt.

Apr 8. Viola hastata. Same field by the brook. Elliott. Pursh. Nutall.

Trillium catesbaei. [name only; three lines blank]

Veronica. (2 new species? No) serpyllifolia. See Elliott Bigelow and particularly the Encyclopaedia in which last the description is perfect. Found by the side of the small streams north of the village. Paul's Betony.

Veronica arvensis. Pursh, Elliott and particularly the Encyclopaedia.
[117]   Leaves aculeate ciliate. I have found no specimens more than an inch and a half or two inches long.

Apr 10. Uvularia sessilifolia. Bigelow. Elliott. Pursh. Distinguished by its branching stem and sessile semiamplexicaule leaves. Has some times more than one flower. See Bigelow. I take the root to be creeping.

Tiarella cordifolia. I think I am not mistaken in this genus by reason of the two unequal pointed styles – and if so there can be no doubt with regard to the species. A future examination of the capsule will decide. The plant agrees perfectly with Pursh except that he does not locate it farther south than Pennsylvania. Pretty well with the Encyclopaedia especially the tuberous, black-fibred root.

Apr 11. Went up the creek from Mr. Kittrells on the farther side. Satisfied myself entirely respecting Anemone nemorosa of which I found much along the shady bank and respecting Staphylea trifolia of which the ["leaves" crossed out] flowers fall almost before they are opened. Found also a plant of the Class Pentandria order Monogynia of which I can make nothing.

Prunus [blank]. Found on this side of the creek. Racemose. Species undetermined.

Ranunculus recurvatus. Pretty common in shady wet places. See Pursh and especially the Encyclopaedia. The only point of difference is that the calix does not appear "pale purplish" that may have been caused by the drying of the specimen in the hands of Dr. Smith. Nor are the petals quite as white or linear as I expected. There can be little doubt.

Apr 12. Down the creek below Mr. Merits. Found an

Anemone [blank]. Not Nos. 1.2.3.4. of Pursh because the leaves are not ternate. Not 5. because the stem is not naked nor the leaves petioled. 6, I have. Not 7. No umbell. Not Nos. 8.9. or 10. - [illegible; "Not"?] of Nutall. leaves not "multifid ["segments" crossed out] leaves 4 or 5.-parted. Segments cuneate." Not 5. because the leaves not ternate. Ergo a new species. *Stem erect 1 to 2 feet high one flowered. With 3 leaves in a whorl.* [illegible word crossed out] *leaves trifid. Segments divaricate smooth. Petals 7.*

[118]   Carpinus vel Ostrya. Genus not fully determined. Fruit to be examined.

Pinus inops. To be farther examined.

Apr 13. Merits Meadow. Several plants about flowering:

Lithospermum arvense. Agrees perfectly with the generic description in the Encyclopaedia and the species well enough with Pursh who is meagre. To be farther examined.

Apr 14. N.W. on Maj. Hendersons and below Prep. School on Mr. Taylors land.

Caprifolium sempervirens. The corollas of the genus are ringent with the exception of No 2. of which it is yellow No doubt.

Uvularia perfoliata. Not flava because the leaves are elliptic not elliptic oval.

Iris cristata. On the bank below the preparatory school house. Certain from the three crested yellow distinct [?] petals.

Found more troublesome Trillium and a plant I do not ascertain.

Apr 15. In a southeasterly direction on Bollings Creek.

Ranunculus fascicularis. That has so long troubled me. determined from Bigelow.

Cerastium glutionosum [sic]. In low damp grounds. Determined from Nutall with whom it agrees perfectly except that I do not find the leaves [illegible] at the ends.

Sisyrinchium anceps. Not gladiatum because the stem is winged and the leaves sword shaped – Neither of them setaceous.

Aesculus [blank]. Not scarlet flowered like pavia – nor downy – like flava – What is it?

Apr 17. S. West on Morgans Creek below Merits.

Hypoxis erecta. Elliott. Pursh. Distinguished from graminea by the shape of the divisions of the corolla. Agrees well with Elliott.

Azalea. [name only; two lines blank at top of next page]

[119]   Viburnum pubescens. East of Merits by the branch. Pursh only. There can be little doubt by reason of the serrate villoso-tomentose leaves. Description might be improved. Leaves heart shaped, nearly sessile with two /linear/ stipules at the bases of each. Calyx purple. and a lin. stip. at base of each stalk /partial flowers/.

Krigia virginica. [name only; one line blank]

Hieracium venosum. Pursh. Bigelow. Not represented as villous as it is sometimes found.

Apr 19. Vaccinium stamineum. Above Kittrells fish traps. There can be little doubt. See Encyclopaedia. The bracteas seem to enlarge as the fruit comes on. Still tis rather corymbose. Fruit to be examined. [Then, in a smaller hand:] [April?] 25. There is no doubt. Bracteas large enough.

Prunus virginiana or serotina? The difference seem to be marked by the leaves and glands of the petioles. We have the single serration of serotina. The smooth midrib of virginiana and the glands are not very regular. Sometimes two on the petiole, sometimes a serration ending in a gland on each side and sometimes both. On Major Henderson's plantation near the house. I am rather inclined to serotina.

Viola. [name only; two lines blank]

Viola ["serpyllifolia" crossed out] /primulifolia/. See Pursh and Elliott Not blanda because the petals are slightly bearded scape and petiole hairy and the former has two glands. Near Mrs. Craig's house.

Apr 20. Merits Meadow.

Rubus trivialis. I am not certainly clear tis not flagellaris. Tis trivialis because tis subpubescent not smooth, recurvato-aculeato hispid – not recurvato aculeate. Petals obovate not orbiculate, – contra. Pedicells sometimes double The time of flowering however agrees with trivialis. There can be little doubt.

Potentilla simplex. But two or at most 3 species are it seems natives [120]   of Carolina. This is determined to a certainty by its rotund-obcordate petals and furthermore by the grossly serrate leaves. Note. The alternate divisions of the calyx narrower. Quest. How the stipules —

Apr 21. North. Found a Gratiola which I cannot make out and also a plant which I believe is a Ranunculus. Mem. The plant by the field side.

Geranium maculatum. [name only]

Phlox nitida /carolina/. These Phloxes plague me. Compare Elliott with Pursh Not acuminata (leaves not thin – calyx not terminating in an awn. Not 3 to 5. feet high E[lliott]). Not paniculata (calix not awned – anthers not linear but large E.) Stem not 3.4. feet high. P[ursh]. Not undulata. calyx not awned, corolla not blue – Not pyramidalis segments of the corolla not wedge shaped truncate. panicle not pyramidal.– Not cordata – no awns no cordate leaves tube of the corolla not 3 times as long as the calix – Not maculata. corymbs not alternate – Not suaveolens corolla not white – Not glaberrima – leaves not linear lanceolate – Not aristata leaves not linear – Not pilosa leaves not linear-lanceolate nor downy – Not amoena – not hirsute – Not divaricata upper leaves not alternate – segments of corolla not obcordate Not reptans – not pubescent or with suckers flowers not blue. Pursh

It must be either carolina or nitida. Disagrees with carolina in not having the corymbs subtrifloris. Agrees perfectly with the nitida of Elliott except that the petals are not retuse and that the petals are of a rose colour.

Crataegus pyrifolia. Near Mr. Norwood's, on New Hope, and I believe on Major Henderson's plantation. Agrees well "spinosa inermisve." The shape also and downiness of the leaves is good and the segments of the calyx linear lanceolate and serrate. The pistils as tis out of flower I cannot well examine.

Apr 24. Below Barbees Mills. Saw a Vaccinium probably – to be remembered.

Smilax rotundifolia. Agrees perfectly except that the leaves are said sometimes to be heartshaped which I do not find. It lies between this and the next and No. 14 from which however it is perhaps sufficiently distinct.

[121]   Ilex prinoides. Pursh. I have little doubt I am right.

Apr 25. West and North. Found a Syngenesious plant – genus not ascertained. Saw a Viburnum to be hereafter examined.

Azalea periclymenoides of Pursh. Nudiflora of Elliott. Elliott and Nutall both complain that Pursh makes species of what are only varieties. ["Pursh" crossed out] Nutall has 6. Distinguished from Nos. 2 and 5. nervo non setigero and from No. 6 by the difference of length in the stamens and tube. Of Nos. 1 and 10 there can be no doubt.

Gratiola virginica. Pursh. Elliott. Agrees with the former except that the leaves are hardly obovate enough or the capsule long enough. Agrees well with Elliott.

Apr 26. Creek above Kittrells.

Morus rubra. Red Mulberry. There can be no doubt of the tree but the flowers and leaves should be again examined as opportunity shall offer.

Phlox aristata vel pilosa. I will not decide till I have more specimens.

Smilacina racemosa. No doubt. Can be confounded only with Number two by reason of its yellowish green flowers and is distinguished from that by the leafy stem. Description good. Pursh.

Andromeda racemosa. The only difficulty was with regard to the linear bracteas at the foot of each peduncle which I now find near the end of the racemes. They are either not constant or deciduous. All along the creek.

Apr 27. Merits Meadow.

Polygala senega – albida of Pursh. alba of Nutall Agrees well with Nutall except that the leaves are not quite as wide as I expected to find 'em.

Coreopsis auriculata Pursh and Encyclopaedia. Agrees well except that the leaves are petioled and the lowest simple. Can [be] little doubt.

Galium uniflorum. Agrees well except that the peduncle is too long. Distinct from all but No. 3 from which it differs in having quaternate cauline leaves.

[122]   **Apr 28.** N. and N. West.

Helonias dioica. There can be no doubt see Elliott.

Magnolia tripetala. Distinguished from M. acuminata by acute instead of obovate petals.

Apr 29. Mr. Lewis's creek.

Houstonia purpurea. No doubt.

Cypripedium. The petals, lip and pubescence agree with this but not the lobe of the style that to [No.] 2.

Galium aparine. [name only]

Viburnum. [name only; two lines blank]

Heuchera americana /viscida/ Pursh. Elliott. Agrees perfectly except that Pursh says the petals are red. Query. A mistake? Not No 2. lobes not acute. Petioles not smooth. Leaves not hispid above. Not 3. leaves not hispido-pilose above Not 4. Not "very villous."

May 1. From Merits down the creek on the other side to the Whetstone Rocks.

Rhododendron punctatum. I am utterly unable to decide whether it be not maximum roseum. The very short calix and ["pink" crossed out] red corolla seem to be decisive, yet the long pedicells and leaves whitish on the under side are opposed. On the whole I think I am right. The habitat of punctatum however seems to be in the mountains on the heads of the great rivers. The same plant I now have grows on the Pilot Mountain.

Euonymus americanus. Pursh. Elliott. Not the least doubt. It may be well however to observe the capsule.

Spiraea trifoliata. Agrees well with Pursh so that I am pretty sure I am right – see also Encyclopaedia. To be sent to Mr. Schweinitz for certainty. Dr. Cave [Dr. Belfield W. Cave, a physician in Chapel Hill; see page 76] says I am right.

Scutellaria serrata. Pursh collated with Nutall. Can be confounded only with No. 9 from which it is probably distinguished by the want of pubescence on the under side of its leaves. See Nutall.

Salvia urticifolia. No doubt.– though the leaves are rhomboidal rather than ovate in the specimen I now have.

[123]   Polygonatum angustifolium. Distinguished from Nos. 2.3.4 and 5 by the sessile not amplexicaule leaves and from No. 6 by the want of an angular stem and ovate leaves.

May 2. Above Kittrells Ford.

Silene antirrhina. Distinguished from all but No. 6 by colour of the flowers and from that by the absence of a spike. Description good except that the leaves are rather linear lanceolate. They are also slightly mucronate – opposite – No doubt.

Euphorbia portulaccoides. It must be of Section II. Not Nos. 4.5.6.– leaves not serrate. Not 7. leaves not linear. Not 8. Agrees perfectly with No. 9 except that No. 9 is marked as found only in Pennsylvania.

Smilax herbacea. Can be confounded only with No. 15 and I am not certain. The nerves, peduncles and umbells agree with this but the shape of the leaves does not. Not thin obtuse to agree with the other. On the whole I am pretty well satisfied but must examine a little farther.

May 3. Bowlings Creek.

Phlox glaberrima. [name only; two lines blank]

Spiraea aruncus. [name only; four lines blank extending into the next page]

[124]   Oenothera sinuata. There can be no doubt. The specific character may rest on the sinuate pinnatfid serrature of the leaves and on the sessile capsules.

May 6. Down the creek opposite Barbees Plantation. Saw in said plantation a Passiflora lutea and another plant in flower which are to be attended to.

Thalictrum rugosum. Dioicous. Certainly a Thalictrum. Not No. 1 because the leaves are 3 lobed not trifid. Not 2.– panicles terminal not axillary. Not 4 from the want of cuneate tomentose leaves. Not 5. leaves not 3 fid. Not 6 – not quinqueffid. Agrees well with rugosum.

Arabis falcata. Agrees perfectly with Pursh except that I cannot from the immature state of the silique determine whether it is "anceps."

Crataegus parvifolia. Remarkable for the lanceolate incised sections of the calyx which it has in common with only one other digynous species. Agrees perfectly except that the leaves are rather obovate than ovate.

May 8. Beyond Craigs. A white syngenesious plant and a shrub not ascertained also another near home.

Penstimon laevigata. Penstimon by reason of the fifth bearded filament exceeding the rest in length. Laevigata by reason of the smooth stalk.

Fedia radiata. Flowers so small I cannot well examine the generic characteristics but the specific are so marked as to leave no doubt.

Sonchus oleraceus. [name only; two lines blank]

Oenothera hybrida Pursh. fruticosa Elliott. Perhaps Nutall. [three lines blank]

[125]   Andromeda mariana. [name only; two lines blank]

Trifolium procumbens. Generally – not always procumbent. Can be confounded only with No. 8 by reason of its yellow flowers. Distinguished from it by its *obovate subemarginate* leaves instead of lanceolate obtuse and also by having the middle one distinctly petioled – the stipules too are short.

May 10. Merits Meadow.

Angelica lucida. The generic character describes angelica as having the involucele as many – at least 8. parted and this has only 5 divisions – yet I am well satisfied I have the angelica both from the opinions of others and the aromatic odour of the root and other characters. Not Cicuta maculata because the veins end in the extremities of the serratures not the sinuses (see Bigelow's Med. Bot.). No good description of it in any of the books. NB leaflets mucronate. Root to be dug up.

Dioscorea villosa. The genus best distinguished by the distant lobes of the anthers – The six divided or 6 leaved calyx without corolla and the habit. Specific character agrees well. Have seen only the male plant.

Erigeron strigosum. Must lie between Nos. 7.8.9.10.11. Certainly not No. 8 because the leaves are not linear lanceolate and perfectly entire. Not No. 9. radical leaves not subrotundo-ovate. Not No. 10 – calyx hemispherical not cylindrical – leaves not ciliate. Not 11. leaves not subulate. It must be No. 7 with which the description agrees well.

Cineraria? [blank] Not in full flower.

May 11. Above Kittrells. Saw 4 plants coming into flower but had bad success in finding flowers expanded.

Bignonia capreolata. No specific character determined by the oblong leaves and smooth stem.

[126]   Crataegus spathulata. Mere guess work.

Allium canadense. Canadense from its bulbiferous head which it has in common only with No. 1 from which it is distinguished by its flat leaves.

May 12. Down the creek about Barbees Mill found either an Andromeda or a Vaccinium and perhaps an Ilex (Ilex prinoides?) about which I am not yet certain.

Agrostemma githago. Common Cockle.

Arum triphyllum. Can be confounded only with No. 3 from which it is distinguished by the length of the spatha doubling that of the spadix.

Vitis aestivilis. Distinguished by the three large distinct lobes and the rufous tomentum of the leaves. My specimen is a male.

Itea virginica. See Elliott and Nutall. Descriptions good. No doubt.

Silene virginica. Distinguished by the deep crimson flowers and oblong leaves.

May 13. Walked with the ladies to the Whetstone Rocks. [In 1820 this was a Saturday]

Smyrnium integerrimum. [name only; one line blank]

May 15. N. West beyond Craigs.

Verbascum blattaria. [name only; one line blank]

Onosmodium hispidum. [name only]

Erigeron heterophyllum. [name only; two lines blank]

Prunella pennsylvanica. [name only]

May 16. Above and below Mr. Kittrells. Saw a plant east of his house coming into flower.

Arum dracontium. [name only]

Kalmia latifolia. [name only; one line blank]

Vitis riparia. [name only; one line blank]

[127]   **May 17.** Merits Meadow.

Senecio balsamitae. Can be confounded only with Cineraria No. 2 and Senecio Nos. 7.9. From the first it is distinguished by its habitat – height – and oblong not spathulate radical leaves. From No. 7. radical leaves not obovate nor crenato-serrate from No. 9. they are far from cordate.– are oblong serrate like balsamitae – The only possible difference is that the stem and peduncles at their base are rather tomentose than villous. No doubt.

Tephrosia virginiana. [name only; one line blank]

Physalis. [name only; four lines blank]

May 18. Maj. Hendersons fields. Saw a Virginia creeper and a plant in the spring coming into flower.

Asclepias variegata. From the colour of the petals and nectaries can be confounded only with Nos. 3.4.5. and 13 – Not 13. leaves neither lanceolate nor sessile. Not 4. leaves not lanceolate nor umbells ["sessile" crossed out] lateral. Not clearly distinguished from Nos. 3. and 5. Stem not weak like 3 nor umbells laxiflores – umbells not lateral like No. 5. and the leaves are too round to agree with either – It has also the rugose leaves and red fructification mentioned by Pursh as belonging to this which the others have not. Very little doubt.

Lysimachia ciliata. Has the ciliate petioles and glandular toothed corolla described by Elliott as belonging to it. There can be little doubt. See Elliott.

Samolus valerandi. The books. Distinguished especially by the 5 scaled corolla and the geniculated bracteated pedicels. No doubt.

Ruellia. [name only; three lines blank]

[128]   Helonias erythrosperma? [name only; three lines blank]

Diospyros virginiana. Persimon tree. Stamina from 8 to 16. Nutall. Distinguished from No. 2 by the smooth oval leaves. Pursh.

May 19. Mr. Taylors Field. Bollings Creek. Plants destroyed by the hail.

Cicuta maculata. [name only; one line blank]

May 20. Creek below Merits. Saw the great thistle of the northern states by the creek and in the road toward Barbees Mill.

Scrophularia marylandica. [name only; one line blank]
Lysimachia quadrifolia. [name only; one line blank]
Azalea viscosa. [name only; two lines blank]
Andromeda paniculata. [name only; three lines blank]
May 22. Major Hendersons field. Saw two or three Asclepias and a shrub.
Marrubium vulgare. White Horehound. On the roads. See particularly the Encyclopaedia in Verbo. No doubt.
Trifolium arvense. Bigelow and Pursh. Common.
Verbena officinalis. spuria of Pursh. I think Nutall may here be a better guide than Pursh. He says the ["officinalis" crossed out] spuria is a mere variety of officinalis. The plant I have can be no other than either the spuria or officinalis and agrees well with the latter but wants the blue corolla of the former. Cannot be hastata on many accounts – its situation on high grounds on the hill &c.
[129]   Rosa. [name only; two lines blank]
May 23. Above and about Kittrells.
Menispermum canadense lobatum. [name only; three lines blank]
Apocynum cannabinum. Pubescens of Elliott. See his References. No doubt. Distinguished by the situation of the cymes, the corolla and the pubescence on the under side of the oblong oval leaves.
Asplenium ebeneum. The first fern I have ascertained. Asplenium from the linear transversal scattered sori – ebeneum – see Pursh and Bigelow. No doubt.
Andromeda speciosa nitida. Description agrees well and I am rendered certain "Antheris apice geminatum 4 aristatis."– Yet my specimen is from a shrub from 6 to 8 feet high and approaches to variety pulverulenta.
May 24. Merits Meadow. Saw a plant in the low ground coming into flower
Cymbidium pulchellum. [name only; two lines blank]
Juncus effusus. [name only; one line blank]
Physalis pubescens. Must be either obscura or ["viscosa crossed out] pubescens of Pursh by reason of the *subcordate ovate orbicular tomentose leaves*. I am inclined to think the obscura pubescens of Pursh and his ["viscosa" crossed out] pubescens are the same plant especially as Elliott says he has specimens of the ["viscosa" crossed out] pubescens from the upper country. The plant I now have is near a foot high. Root fusiform? Stem branched with two great branches. Stem and leaves very ["villous" crossed out] pubescent and viscid, leaving an oil on the fingers after handling.– leaves ovate cordate acuminate generally two together with one larger /yellowish green/. Petioles 1 to 2 inches long. Flowers axillary pendulous. peduncles / 1/2 / an inch to /an inch/ long, segments of the calyx subulate,* as long or longer than the petals. Petals yellow /segments 3 lobed/ with large brown spots at the base said spots villous at the bottom /along the lower edge/. Stamens deep purple half as long as the corolla. Anthers light purple. Plant stinking.
[Footnote added at bottom of page] *Not always. Sometimes much shorter. Anthers yellow. Leaves dentate orbicular.
[130]   **May 29.** Major Hendersons field. Saw some plants coming into flower.
Pteris aquilina. Pursh's description is copied from Willdenow on the European plant and is therefore good for nothing. See Bigelow who is pretty good.
Cornus sericea. I am not very certain and shall tell better when I have seen more species. It has the leaves of sericea perfectly and the fructification is perfectly cymose but they [sic] cymes are convex. No.
Jun 10. N. West but was shortly obliged to return by rain.
Yucca filamentosa. From Mrs. Caldwells garden but I recollect having seen it

on Bald Head Mountain near the G. Falls of the Yadkin. Can be confounded only with the angustifolia of the Missouri which is also stemless. Bear Grass.

Lobelia cliffortiana? [name only; three lines blank]

Scutellaria integrifolia. Distinguished from all but Nos. 4 and 6 by the narrow leaves and from No. 4 by the racemose flowers. It is probably the same with No. 4.

Verbena rugosa. Tis of Section 2nd by reason of the entire leaves and rugosa by reason of its height – 1 foot – its linear lanceolate leaves rugose and serrate and by the filiform terminal and axillary spikes. No doubt.

Scorzonera pinnatifida. Description good. Common in cultivated fields.

Troximon virginicum. A good deal resembling a K[r]igia.

Polygala incarnata. Distinguished by its simple stalk and subulate leaves.

Gnaphalium uliginosum. [name only; five lines blank]

[131]   **Jun.** Back of Kittrells. Crossed the creek at the usual place. Went to McCauleys and came in the road home.

Gonolobus ["hispidus" crossed out] hirsutus. Pursh. Determined as yet by the dark brown lanceolate leaves of the corolla and the ovate cordate acuminate pubescent leaves. The follicles are to be hereafter examined. Probably the hirsutus of Pursh and the macrophyllus of Elliott.

Jun 13. To Major Hendersons fields. Saw a good many plants coming into flower, in particular a certain succulent one in Craigs field.

Asclepias viridiflora obovata. Is certainly a viridiflora by reason of the colour of the fructification and the upright hornless nectaries but it agrees not in regard to the leaves. Probably the same with the obovata of Elliott and has as good a right to be a distinct species as the lanceolata of Ives.

Ludwigia palustris. Elliott, lucida of Pursh. Certain. Tis of Section first by reason of the want of petals and cannot be the others by reason of size habit or shape of leaves. It agrees also perfectly in situation &c except that the leaves are rather ovate than lanceolate.

Prinus verticillata? Agrees well except that the leaves are ["oval" crossed out] lanceolate rather than oval and the flowers hermaphrodite. Great doubt. The shrub found some time ago and thought an Ilex probably belongs to this genus.

[132]   Phleum pratense. Timothy. Herds Grass. Description good. Glumes [illegible] on the back with two short awns. Introduced.

Psoralea mellilotoides. One is not much the wiser for the generic character but as this is founded on the capsule it may be well to examine this hereafter to see whether it agrees. The specific character is so distinct and marked that there can be no doubt. See Pursh.

Lysimachia heterophylla? This Lysimachia I have found both here and at Salem in dry situations. About 18 inches high erect branched lower leaves opposite ovate lanceolate. The upper not much differing in shape – rather narrower in 4's. Peduncles shorter than the leaves. Leaves mucronate. Segments of the calyx lanceolate – of the corolla orbiculo-mucronate and serrulate at the end. Stamens hairy. Nearly allied to ciliata. Question. A variety?

Galium circaezans. Pursh & Elliott. Distinguished by its uncinato-hispid fruit. by the lateral and terminal fructification and nodding fruit and the ovate ciliate obtuse three-ne[r]ved leaves. Very little doubt.

Bromus secalinus. Found in rye fields. See the books. Description good. Notandum the calyx and glume.

Pycnanthemum. [name only; two lines blank]

Jun 14. Merits Meadow by the way of Kittrells brook.

Stylosanthes hispida erecta Mr. Schweinitz. Many things about it agree very well but that the corolla is is [*sic*] inserted on the calyx as says the generic character is not so clear. The stalk instead of being hispid on one side is sometimes hispid and sometimes smooth. The leaves are sometimes ciliate.

Tragia urticifolia. Certainly a Tragia. The leaves are hardly broad enough for urticifolia but the deep serratures and hispid stalk put it beyond debate.

Anemone virginica. From the dichotomal stalk and the leaves – "ternis, ternatis, trilobis" no doubt.

[133] (as branching from the pedicell'd round fructification. Yet the pinnulae are lobed! [This seems to pertain to a fern, yet it has no obvious connection to *Osmunda spectabilis*, which follows it on the page.]

Osmunda spectabilis. Section three of the Cryptogamous plants. Differs I believe from Section Fourth in having the fructification on a different stalk or different part of the stalk instead of the back. Must be.

Lycopodium apodum. (Mr. Schweinitz.) Pursh. From the shape of the leaves. – their being in two rows and from No.12 by the habitat. Carolina.

(Hepaticae) Marchantia polymorpha. Mere guesswork from the plant being called Liverwort. To be sent to Mr. Schweinitz.

Monotropa lanuginosa. Pursh Elliott. Good except that it seems frequently octandrous and the corolla 8 leavd. Only the upper part is downy.

Castanea chinquapin. Distinguished from vesca by having the underside of the leaf white and downy.

Polygala ["chinquapin" crossed out] verticillata. Agrees in the branching stem linear leaves and the alternate flowers on a long spike as also in their colour, but only the lower leaves amounting to 4 or 5 or verticillate not on the spikes as I see setaceous. It must lie between this – the next and a new species. Not the next certainly from the flowers not being in sessile heads. Rather uncertain.

[June 21, 1820. A note with this date in Mitchell's copy of Pursh, p. 182, under *Asclepias amplexicaulis*, gives the locality "Near M. . " (illegible)].

Jun 27. List of plants found about Hillsborough from the time of my coming hither June 17 up to this day. [This list of 20 species, name only, continues through page 134 to the top of 135].

Achillea millefolium [one line blank]
Teucrium virginicum [one line blank]
Calcalia [*sic*] atriplicifolia [one line blank]
Ferula villosa [one line blank]
Verbena urticifolia [one line blank]
Justicia pedunculosa [two lines blank]
[134] Lactuca elongata [one line blank]
Isanthus coeruleus [two lines blank]
Geum virginianum [three lines blank]
Chimiphila [*sic*] maculata [one line blank]
Coreopsis verticillata [one line blank]
Aster conyzoides [two lines blank]
Polypodium hexagonopterum [four lines blank]
Oxalis dillenii? [two lines blank]
Saururus cernuus

Bignonia radicans
Cnicus lanceolatus [one line blank]
Cuphaea viscosissima [one line blank]
Hypericum corymbosum [one line blank]
[135] Aletris alba [one line blank]
Clitoria mariana [one line blank]
Jun 27. Mr Yarboroughs meadow.

Stachys hispida. Generic description agrees well, also the specific. Can be confounded only with aspera. Distinguished by the leaves & calyx.

Linum virginicum. Pentandria pentagyinia. From the colour of the flowers and the leaves.

Melanthium virginicum. Melanthium from the claws of the corolla bearing the stamens. Virginicum from the hastate petals with long claws and from the flowers being generally hermaphrodite. Also the habitat.

Bartsia coccinea. Descriptions good. Tis the plant with crimson floral leaves I used to admire so much in the meadows.

Phlox maculalata [*sic*]. [name only; one line blank]
Aster puniceus. [name only; one line blank]
Orchis psycodes. [name only; one line blank]

[136][List of nine species with no localities cited; perhaps a later addition].

Mimulus alatus [name only; one line blank]
Sabbatia angularis [name only; one line blank]
Penthorum sedoides [name only; one line blank]
Ludwigia decurrens [name only; one line blank]
Vernonia novebor[ac]ensis [name only; two lines blank]
Pycnanthemum incanum [name only; two lines blank]
Oenothera muricata [name only; one line blank]
Orchis ciliaris [name only; two lines blank]
Sabbatia corymbosa [name only; two lines blank]

[137]   **Aug 1.** Through the Presidents field and down the branch.

Galactia mollis. A vine common in all dry fields. Galactia from the 4 cleft calyx and the bracteas. Mollis from the pubescence unemarginate leaves elongated raceme and compressed legume. See Nutall.

Crotolaria sagittalis. Certainly a Crotolaria. Not clear of the species. The leaves are lanceolate and the flowers large which is good. The stipule is a wing on each side of the branch ending upwards in a point.

Rhexia mariana rubella. From the round hirsute stem and rose coloured flowers.
Phryma leptostachia. No doubt, especially from the declining calyx.
Gerardia flava. [name only; one line blank]
Eupatorium rotundifolium. The shape of the leaves – leaves no doubt.

Hedysarum nudiflorum. Certain – from the fructification being on a scape distinct from the leaf bearing stem and the loments.

Aug 2. Mr. Taylor's field below the Prep. School house.
Sida spinosa. Description Pursh agrees perfectly with this and no other species.
Mollugo verticillata. Pursh. Generic and specific description both good.
Spermacoce diodina. The common plant so much resembling a Diodia.
Erigeron canadense. The tall plant I have sometimes called Wild Hemp.

Polymnia uvedalia. Polymnia from the peculiar double calyx. Uvedalia from the uniformly 3 lobed decurrent leaves.

Passiflora lutea. Lutea from the petals and leaves.

Lycopus virginicus. [name only; one line blank]

Agrimonia eupatoria. See Bigelow. Description agrees well. Distinguished from the other two species by the shape of its leaves (obovate).

Aug 7. Bidens bipinnata. In the garden. Bidens from the generic description. Bippinata from being semiradiate – the bipinnate leaves with the folioles pinnatifid – though they are generally pinnate with the folioles bipinnatifid. It can however be no other.

Amaranthus hybridus. The specimen I have is pentandrous and is therefore [138] after No. 5. in Pursh. with ovate leaves therefore not No. 10. The axills not spinous therefore not No. 11. Not No. 8 certainly as it has neither smooth branches supradecomposite racemes nor oblong acute leaves. Not Nos. 7.9. from the want of supradecomposite racemes – spreading branches and undulate leaves. Agrees well with hybridus. See Bigelow.

Polygonum mite. The spike is not slender enough nor the flowers purple enough. But the leaves, the ochreae and the bracteae agree perfectly. Flowers to be examined.

Chenopodium botrys. The terminal racemes the smell and the oblong sinuate leaves which are rather profundissime pinnatifid determine the plant. See Eaton. In the garden.

Cassia chamaecrista. Must be of the 4 last by reason of the number of leaves. From the stamens and the gland cannot be of the two last and from the large spotted flowers and ["many flowered" crossed out] /2 or 3/ fascicles. Not No.7.

Eupatorium album. A common but very difficult plant. If by coloratis he means albis I am certainly right. Why the name albis if he does not. The rest of the description agrees perfectly. See also falcatum in Michaux. I am pretty certainly right. It must lie between Nos. 7.8.9.10.11.13. Not 8. "Calycinis squamis concoloribus." Pursh. Not 9. "Folia erecta; e latiora basi sensim acuta" /Nut/ Not 10. Foliis obovato-lanceolatis apice subserratis triplinervibus: Not above a foot high. Pursh. Not 11. "foliis. glabriusculis. Resembles No 9." Pursh Not 13 – of this I am not clear.

Mikania scandens. I[s] certainly a Mikania and agrees well with the description of the scandens. Flowers purple and odorous.

Heliotropium indicum. On the hill. A great stinkard. See Pursh Elliott.

Hedysarum viridiflorum. Must be of Nos. 5.7. or 15. from the oval shape of the loments. Not 15. from the shape of its leaves. Not 7. from its pubescence.

Aster ericoides. [name only; two lines blank]

Solidago latifolia. See Encyclopaedia.

[139] [On the next several pages there follows a list of seven names without commentary and eleven with commentary, interspersed with some paragraphs on ancient Greece and the "Calendar of Flora" that Mitchell kept briefly in February and March of 1820 (see above, p. 32). All but two of the other plant entries are undated, but mostly the species are summer or fall flowering and appear to follow naturally after page 138].

Cassia nictitans
Clitoria virginiana [one line blank]
Hieracium gronovii (foliosum) [two lines blank]

Hedysarum paniculatum [three lines blank]
Eupatorium purpureum [two lines blank]
Lobelia cardinalis [two lines blank]
Rudbeckia digitata. I have a Rudbeckia. [two lines blank]
Inula graminifolia. My species lies betwen graminifolia and argentea (see Nutall) by reason of its silky covering. Is the former by reason of its glandular calyx and its small flowers. See Pursh. On dry knolls in the woods.

[Eight lines on ancient Greece on this page, and nine lines at the top of page 140.]

[140]   Hyssopus nepetoides. I am pretty sure I am right from the generic and specific characters but how of "Stylis corolla brevioribus" M. To find.

Heliopsis laevis. Has long plauged [sic] me. Very much resembles an Helianthus. Has a good deal the calyx of a Silphium. I have no doubt respecting it. Common in cultivated fields.

Conyza camphorata. A plant every one will be anxious to get rid of as soon as he can. Somewhat resembles an Eupatorium. The species can be confounded only with No. 1 from which it is distinguished by its size and habitat. See Nutall.

Clematis virginica. The plant I have is a male. By reason of the ternate leaves it can be confounded only with holosericea from which it is distinguished by the shape of the leaves. The description agrees well. Found Aug. 15. Merits Meadow at the crossing place.

Helenium autumnale. Merits Meadow. Agrees well with both the generic and specific description – especially the trifid rays. There seems to be very little difference betwixt this and the succeeding [presumably referring to the sequence of species given in Pursh, Elliott, or someother flora] and I suspect them to be the same.

Scutellaria lateriflora. Very distinct by its ovate petiolate leaves and lateral leafy racemes of small flowers. Same place. Aug. 15.

Dracocephalum virginianum. Distinguished from denticulatum by its thick flowered spike linear lanceolate leaves and tall stalk.

Lespedeza sessiliflora. Erect. Therefore of the three first. Not polystachya by reason of the leaves. Not capitata by reason of the shortness of the calyx. "Calycibus villosis longitudine corollae" (capitata)

[141]   Liatris squarrosa. By reason of its having but 3 or 4 flowers on a stalk and its long grassy leaves it must be of Nos. 3.6.7.8. ["9" crossed out] or 12. (See Pursh). Not 7 or 8. amongst other good reasons because of the number of florets in a calyx (see Nuttall [sic]) 8–10. My specimen has 28. Nor 6 for the same reason (see Pursh) and from the calyx leaves. Not 3. "Calycinis squamis oblongis obtusis mucronatis ciliatis *appressis*." Agrees well with squarrosa in Pursh very well with Nutall and if the florets be villous within the description will be perfect and I have no doubt now.

Xyris caroliniana. Somewhat like a bulbous L? Yellow flowers in heads. [two lines blank]

Aug 17. Through Mr. Kittrells fields. Mem. The plant believed a Liatris, the Gerardia quercifolia. Sonchus sp.

Helianthus decapetalus. Helianthus from the "Pappus diphylus." Agrees well with this species.

Helianthus atrorubens. See Pursh. Disk not as dark a purple as I expected.

Helianthus macrophyllus. Is of Nos. 13 or 14 from the leaves. scabrous above and downy below. Macrophyllus from the squarrose calyx.

Tephrosia hispidula. No doubt. Description agrees well with Pursh.

[142]   Polygonum virginianum. From its virgate raceme and ovate lanceolate leaves. See also Elliott.

Sida abutilon. 14 pistils. Abutilon from the shape of the leaves – round cordate. The two aristae in the green capsule appear as one.

Inula mariana. Can be no other species. Pursh. Agrees perfectly except that the leaves are rather acute.

Mimulus ringens. Description agrees perfectly. Pursh.

["Gnaphalium germanicum" crossed out]

Aug 18. Mrs. Craig's field.

Eclipta ["procumbens" crossed out] erecta. A very [illegible] plant. Generic description agrees well (See Encyclopaedia). I am uncertain whether I have not the ["erecta" crossed out] procumbens. "Strigosa" "pedunculis geminis" seem to point to this. "Dichotoma," "foliis lanceolatis" as opposed to "longo-lanceolatis," "calyicinis [sic] foliolis ovatis," "in dry gravelly soil," throw it on the other. Perhaps what makes for is more decisive than what makes against. Query. Is it erect or decumbent?

Chenopodium anthelminticum. Description good. See Elliott.

Gratiola acuminata. See Elliott whose description is good.

[143]   **Sep 4.** Returned from Hillsborough where I found certain plants in Mr. Yarborough's meadow on Saturday last. [In 1820, September 2 was a Saturday.]

Cnicus muticus. A tall thistle. Must be of Nos. 2.3.4. or 5. Not No. 3, which is the Canada Thistle found only in the northern states and so troublesome there – Not No. 5. which is simple – having commonly but one flower. Not 2 of which leaves are only "levissime obtuseque sinuosis" (M[ichau]x.). Agrees so well with No. 4 that I have no doubt though the scales of the calyx are some of them slightly mucronate and the calyx itself ventricosus.

Aconitum uncinatum. A strange looking flower the pistils of which I did not observe.

Sium tricuspidatum (Elliott). The specific description is such as to leave no doubt. The seeds are almost smooth.

Eupatorium altissimum. The description agrees well except that the lower leaves are rather "apice serratis" than "medio serratis."

Chelone glabra. With a flower like a snake's head. No doubt.

Apios frutescens. Wisteria. Speciosa of Nutall who gives a long description – correct except that the leaves are not always in fives. On Dr. Webbs arbour. I know not whence it came.

Eupatorium linearifolium. Can be confounded only with No. 3 from which it is distinguished by its leaves and dotted calyx. Found about the Devil's Turnip Patch on the road to Hillsborough.

Cassia marylandica. Distinguished by its fructification and foliis 8 jugis. Grows near Watson's shop.

Monotropa uniflora. Distinguished from morisoniana by its cernuous flower.

Sep. 5, 1820 [!]. Dr. Caldwell's field towards Kittrells.

Gerardia quercifolia. Pursh's description and figure leave no doubt.

Aster phlogifolius. The leaves are broad, entire and amplexicaule which throws it between Nos. 30, 35, 36. Not 30. "Calycinis squamis laxis linearibus acutis *aequalibus.*" Not 36. Calyx not spreading. Agrees well with this.

Solidago procera. Is of the first 7 in Pursh. Not 1 or 3. by reason of the habitat. Not 4. leaves very distinctly three nerved. Not ciliate (5) – "Ramis reflexis."

[144]   (6) Not "Racemis subrecurvis." (7). Agrees well with procera especially the spiked branches.

Solidago patula. Is of Section 2, and by reason of the form of the leaves is between Nos. 14 and 15. The gray aspect and roughish leaves look to No. 14. The spathulate serrate leaves to No. 15. Uncertain.

Phaseolus perennis. Is a Phaseolus. Agrees well with perennis and can be no other by reason of the broad legume.

Hedysarum glabellum. I rather think we have 8. Hedysarums that are common. Nudiflorum paniculatum, and viridiflorum already described. and canescens; obtusum glabellum bracteosum & rotundifolium Not described. Of these canescens. obtusum and glabellum are nearly related. Also viridiflorum and bracteosum. The rest are sufficiently distinct.

[At some point after writing these lines Mitchell keyed out another species of *Hedysarum*. The passage is not dated, but the handwriting is certainly of the 1820s rather than the 1830s.]

[189]   Hedysarum obtusum. Elliott gives 17 Hedysarums. Of these. 1.4.5.8 .9.10. 11.13.15.16. = ten in all are thrown out by the shape of the joints of the loment triangular and rhomboidal. 1 is also thrown out because known. 4 by its narrow leaves.– 8. known – prostrate 9. bracteas large. 10 leaves oblong lanceolate. 11 leaves villous underneath – 12 bracteas ovate lanceolate. 13. bracteas *ovate* acuminate 15. leaves *villous* and *very soft underneath*. 16. bracteas ovate. so that all except 5 are distinct clearly by a second character besides that of the loment. and even 5 is pretty distinct.

2. is laid out by its *terminal panicle* and by being sprinkled all over with soft hair. 3 by its *linear leaves*. 12 by *leaves 2 inches long. 5–7 lines wide – thick*. 14 by leaves.– *rhomboidal obtuse thick rugose*. 17. by its *creeping stem* There remain only 6 and 7. of which the distinct characters are as follow.

obtusum leaves. *obtuse. slightly cordate at base stipules subulate* [*obtusum* is No. 6 in Elliott and *ciliare* is No. 7]

ciliare. leaves *pubescent underneath fringed along the margin*. I find the lowest two rather than three jointed but on the whole have little doubt I am right.

[145]   **Sep 8.** North of the village.

Aster ericoides. Lies between Nos. 13.14.15 on account of either the height of the plant which is frequently 3 or 4 feet, the colour of the disk and ray which are yellow and nearly white and the linear leaves of the stalk and the subulate leaves on the branches and by reason of the subsquarrose calyx it is ericoides.

Dec 15, 1820 [!]. It may now be proper to make the last botanical note that I shall probably write this year. I have within a week received some new books from which I have ascertained some new trees.

Juglans tomentosa. Near Mr. Taylors. Determined by the nut only to my entire satisfaction. It may not however be improper to look at the leaves.

Juglans porcina. Close by the corner of our yard. By the fruit. No doubt.

Quercus aquatica. Michaux, Sylva. Abundant by the creek toward Barbees Mill.

Quercus nigra. Common Black Jack.

Pinus variabilis. Common yellow pine. From its double leaves and from Michauxs account of the localities of the other two leaved species it can be no other.

[146]   In about 6 weeks the new botanical campaign will commence. I must not then forget the field where the old Indian settlements were with its willows not [sic] the two elms near Kittrells ford.

[The following entry is undated as to year. Because it uses Smith but not Bridel to identify a species of moss, we have concluded that it must be earlier than November 1821, when Mitchell received a copy of Bridel that would thereafter be his first resource in studying the mosses; indeed, in that month he shows himself already familiar with the moss identified in this entry. In January 1820 Mitchell had not yet begun seriously to examine the flowering plants, let alone the mosses, and it seems more plausible to date this entry to 1821. He began his study of the flowering plants a month later.]

[99] Muscologia Mons-Sacelliensis
Jan. 8 [1821?]. Went below the Preparatory School House and brought 4 mosses.
Polytrichum undulatum. The capsules are now ripe. Is perfectly and well determined from Smith. by the leaves. somewhat pellucid undulate serrate — the serratures carnose (See No. 1 Page 14 line 4.) the calyptra with its extremity roughened as by rudiments of setae the mouth of the capsule red and larger than the body.

1821 [!]

Feb 5. Alnus serrulata. Common Black Alder. The only species in the Southern States. Was found so far advanced as to shed its pollen by the side of Kittrells ford. The first tree that blooms with us. The flowers of Ulmus americana have burst from their scales but are not yet opened.

[Comments on *Alnus serrulata, Ulmus americana, Draba verna,* and *Draba hispidula*, from February 5, 9, and 12, 1821, were rewritten in greater detail on p. 207 and are interspersed here in the appropriate positions.]

[207] Alnus serrulata. Common Black Alder. A common well known shrub growing in wet miry places and by the sides of small branches. It is sometimes 10 feet high and 2 inches thick. Leaves round-oval, doubly denticulated. The twin twigs at the extremities of the branches bear the long pendulous [illegible word crossed out] aments /of [illegible] flowers/ and [illegible word crossed out] fertile cones which appear long before the leaves. Febry. 5, 182[1]. Flowered. The fertile cones remain after the scales have fallen.
Ulmus americana. A pretty large tree growing in wet places. The branches are long and pendulous. The buds are conical, having the flowers enveloped in sheathing scales. In the axil of each scale is a peduncle bearing two or 3 flowers. When the flower bursts out the scales drop and there is a little bunch of flowers. The ["fruit is" crossed out] seed is contained in what is called a samara on a long peduncle. ["leaves" crossed out] It is flat winged fringed at the edges and notched at the end. Ripens in May? Leaves alternate, doubly denticulated, unequal at base. Near Mr. Taylors. Some flowers had burst from their scales and were nearly opened. Febry. 5, 1821 [!]. White Elm.
[146] **Feb 9, 1821** [!]. Draba verna. Satisfactorily ascertained from Nutall and Pursh by the general description of leaves stalk and time of flowering and more especially the bifid petals. Silicula to be hereafter examined. It had apparently just come into flower. Saw an Acer – not rubrum which is to be watched.
[207] Draba verna. Copy ["Nutall" crossed out] Barton who seems to be perfect unless there be something to add on the score of the silicule. It seems to me rather to prefer a damp soil. Just flowered Feb. 9. 1821 [!].

[146] **Feb 10.** A ride down to Barbees Mill and the creek below. Satisfied myself that both Carpinus americana and Ostrya virginica are found with us. Saw some oaks that are to be watched. Cactus opuntia on a rock. Reeds by the creek side and some droll trees. A maple in flower as I came home. Acer rubrum.

Feb 12. Draba hispidula. Pursh. Michaux. Michaux is the best by far. I have no doubt. Upper end of Merit's Meadow.

[207] Draba hispidula. Lately flowered. In flower Febry. 12. with some /very short/ leafy branches purplish, giving of[f] at the extremity a naked peduncle. Petals larger than in the last [= Draba verna]. Leaves oval, acutish, /very/ hirsute, sometimes with a tooth or two. Silicule? 2 to 6 inches high.

[146] **Mar 2.** After a long interval I at length make a record. Have paid some attention to the mosses. Prunus chicasa had a few flowers expanded as early as the 22 Febry. Amygdalus persicaria do. about March 1. Prunus now in full flower. Only here and there a limb of the peach expanded. Erythronum lanceolatum and Saxifraga virginiensis in flower as early as 18th Febry.

Poa annua. Elliott. Encyclopaedia. No doubt from the generic description which I now understand, time of flowering &c. Common. The earliest spring grass. Found a fern I did not ascertain. Poa annua one of the first grasses ascertained. Proprio Marte [This very March].

[147] **Apr 21.** From Merits Meadow up to the Maples at the turn of Creek. Found Orontium aquaticum, Pedicularis canadensis, Viburnum —, Potentilla simplex and Arum triphyllum. A plant at the bend not ascertained. Saw also Sysirinchium anceps and Hypoxis erecta.

Aira melicoides. Pretty well ascertained sometime ago. Agrees with Elliotts triflora except that in no instance do I find three flowers or a pubescence at the bottom of the corolla.

Stipa avenacea. Pursh and Elliott. There is a pretty small beard at the base of the corolla. Tis rather hair.

Viola striata. The only white violet with a stem. A good beard on the lateral petals. Procumbent agrees not with Elliott. At the Maples.

Viola pubescens. Agrees with Pursh and can be no other as hastata is already ascertained. The lateral petals slightly bearded and the lower with streaks of purple; flowers small. Same place.

Chaerophyllum claytoni. Separated into a new genus by Nutall. Uraspermum. Nutalls description gives all can be desired. Same place.

Oxalis corniculata about which I had some doubts [see Mar. 29, 1820] is known by its early flowering and semi-procumbent habit.

Myosotis arvensis. Which I last year [see Apr. 13, 1820] called a Lithospermum now ascertained by comparing Pursh and Barton.

Arabis lyrata. A plant common in the cultivated fields along Merits Creek having compressed siliquae I have concluded to call by this name because I can call it nothing else. Possibly right.

Ellisia nyctelea. I was well satisfied about this plant before except that I could not make the loculi and seeds of the capsule agree. But I have now two valves and 3 seeds. I assume there are 4 when the plant is perfect — I found two Carexes making 4 species quite distinct I have found this year but I call no names as yet. Ellisia is at the corner of the fence near the Maples.

Apr 23. Mr. Taylors field. Saw Trillium catesbaei, Phlox nitida, Tiarella cordifolia, Cerastium (Nutall) in flower. Sundry grasses coming.

Ranunculus recurvatus. Not Nos.11.12.13.14.18.20.21.22.23. because the leaves
[148] are neither ternate or capillaceous. Not Nos. 6.7.8.10.20. because not

smooth. Is therefore either (auricomus – acris – lanuginosus – tomentosus or recurvatus). Not acris which is 2 feet high (Ency). Not lanuginosus which has the height and large petals of acris – Not tomentosus as it is many flowered. Not auricomus – the kidney shaped leaves and time of flowering agree well, but not the "hardly downy except near the top" nor "Flowers of a bright golden hue." There remains only recurvatus, agrees in everything except its location in shady woods.

Finally I am uncertain. It is possible it may be auricomus. It may be that Pursh and Dr. Smith mean different things by lanuginosus and that I have the lanuginosus of Pursh – or I may have the recurvatus. Tis common everywhere at this season covering the commons and lying close to the ground. It however affects damp places. The plant from 4 to 6 inches high. flowers very inconspicuous, the leaves and stalk covered with a soft silky down which renders the specimen I have – taken from low grounds one of the softest plants I ever felt.

Viola sagittatta emarginata. Nutall. Distinguished by its leaves and emarginate petals. grows abundantly along the road by Barbees plantation this side of his mill.

An umbellate plant and a small tree perhaps an Ilex unascertained.

Apr 24. Have been puzzling my head with the Poae. There is one now in flower in shady places in my garden which I canot make out. It has been in flower I believe a good while. 4 to 6 inches high, leaves 1-2 inches long. Spikelets 3 and 4 flowered anthers yellowish stigmas feathered.

Poa annua. I had suspected from the descriptions of Elliott and Barton and the habitat as given by Elliott it was the annua. But Muhlenburg gives entire satisfaction especially characters 6.7.8.9. which leave no doubt. Found in my garden.

[It may have been at this time that Mitchell drew up a synoptic table, characterizing about 30 species of *Poa*, a composite made up of data from the works of Torrey, Muhlenberg, and Elliott. The table appears on pages 16 and 17 of his ledger. He was then stimulated to describe what he took to be a new species]:

[17]   Poa stricta Mihi. Culm 2–3 feet high – smooth, round. Stem leaves 4–6 inches long, 2 lines wide, smooth on the ["upper" crossed out] lower surface, scabrous on the ["lower" crossed out] upper.– Sheath 4–6 inches long – smooth. Stipules very small. Panicle 6–8 inches long. Capillary – Branches geminate, distant – 1–2 inches – (10–12) long, appressed, nutant (?), /flexuous, scabrous,/ subdivided; ["flowers" crossed out] spikes few – 3–4 flowered, fasciolate. Calyx leaves lanceolate acute, the upper a little the largest, whitish on the margin – quite scabrous on the back. Corolla scabrous (so that if a small knife be drawn over it a very distinct sound will be heard), whitish and membranaceous on the margin – [illegible: ?lamina] very short (I have never seen the anthers outside of the corolla) – Anthers yellowish; stigmas white, feathery, small.

Grows on the margins of woods generally in the shade, very erect, colour dark green. Panicle fully formed but it has not flowered.

Poa stolonifera Muhlenburg.

[148]   **May 2.** I have made no entries for some time.

Crataegus apiifolia. I begin to get acquainted with the genus /See April 21, 1821 [!] [this insertion, apparently in a later hand, is evidently mistaken as to year: on Apr 21, *1820*, Mitchell referred to *Crataegus pyrifolia*] / Crataegus. The apiifolia is quite distinct by its "Oblong calyx – Deltoid – inciso-lobate leaves" "Molli et candicanti lanugine conspersa." M[ichau]x.

[149]   Crataegus spathulata. Not yet in flower.

Crataegus crus galli. On the road to New Hope. To be examined next year. Beyond N. Hope and near Hillsboro plenty April 29 in flower. Certain from the corymbs. (See Nos. 8.9). Subserrate leaves of the calyx (No. 10). ["foliis" crossed out] *eglandulosis* petiolis No. 7.

Crataegus parvifolia. Not in flower.

Crataegus coccinea. From the smooth leaves and five pistils is either of No. 3 or 4. The fruit chiefly will decide which is to be examined. Below Barbees Mill.

Phlox pilosa. Certainly the pilosa of Elliott which I suspect to be the aristata of Pursh and vice versa.

[150]   **May 24.** Picked up the following in Dr. Caldwells yard.

Physalis lanceolata. 6 or 8 inches high. Stem and leaves – stem especially – villoso-pubescent. *Stem* /not always/ purplish – in one specimen trichotomal with one branch dichotomal, the other specimen twice dichotomal. Peduncles axillary 3/4 of an inch to an inch long. Calyx villous hemispherical half as long as the corolla. Corolla yellow with brown spots alternating with the anthers – between each brown spot there is a yellow line, the bottom of the corolla villous. The stamens and style dark purple approaching to blue – the anthers whitish with a shade of blue especially after bursting. The leaves single at the dichotomal peduncle, double on the branches, ovate, not approaching to cordate – pubescent slightly viscid with something like 2 or three large irregular toothings on each side. Fruit or berry?

May 25. Dug up a plant of the above species and found from the root that it is perennial. Stamens smooth; not half the length of the corolla. As being perennial it must according to Elliott be the lanceolata of Michaux and of course of Pursh who either had never seen the species living or called it by some other name. I am very glad to arrive at anything like certainty respecting this plant. Yet I think there is another perennial species.

Physalis pubescens. I am getting hold of this genus. Perennial. My present specimen is about a foot high but is not yet mature. Yellowish green. The last was of a dark green – is a much more robust plant. The root is as large as my finger and runs perpendicularly and deeply into the earth. villoso pubescent and very viscous leaving an oil on the fingers. Stems twice dichotomal. Flower calyx and flower smaller than in the last. Leaves cordate ovate irregularly toothed – plant very stinking. flower not yet expanded.

May 30 or June [sic]. I have to day found as I think the last of the oaks that I shall find in this neighbourhood. The species are twelve in number within 2 miles of the hill [this last sentence is essentially the same as one in Mitchell's letter to Schweinitz in June 1821]. Two I have noted already some pages back but it may not be amiss to set them all down together with the places where they grow observing that I have no doubt respecting any of them. I must still be on the lookout in the swamps for Q. prinus discolor.

[151]   Quercus alba. In the grove – Common every where. White oak. [The "grove" was the uncut, forested part of the university land, especially between the existing buildings and Franklin Street.]

Quercus obtusifolia. The same. Post oak.
Quercus tinctoria. The same. Black oak.
Quercus coccinnea. The same. Scarlet oak.
Quercus nigra. The same. Black jack.
Quercus falcata. The same. Spanish oak.

Quercus phellos. On the left hand of the road to Maj. Hendersons plantation. Willow oak.

Quercus aquatica. On the creek between Merit and Barbees mills. Water oak.

Quercus prinus palustris. Kittrells ford. Chestnut white oak.

Quercus prinus monticola. Laurel Hill above Kittrells on the creek. Rock oak.

Quercus lyrata. In wet places in front of the last. Overcup oak.

Quercus rubra. One stock at Barbees eastern mill. Red oak.

[June 17, 1821. A note of this date in Mitchell's copy of Pursh, p. 107, under *Ptelea trifoliata*, gives the locality, "Col. Jones Plantation."]

[151]   **Sep 5** [immediately following the list of oaks but in a different ink]. Iterum "χαιρετε" studia dilecta nimium neglecta. [Once again, rejoice! Back to my beloved too much neglected studies.]

Paspalum floridanum. Major Hendersons field beyond Craigs. The plant I have been accustomed to call the floridanum must give way to this. First by reason of the size. It is sometimes six feet. Nex[t] by the various other descriptions which agree well. Stigmas feathery, almost black. Anthers a chocolate.

[184]   **Oct 16.** Have been all day to day engaged in preparing my plants to be sent up to Mr. Schweinitz. Have resolved to lay it down as a rule that Wednesdays and Saturdays are to be devoted to botany. I will here note the criticisms I make on my plants as I look them over–

Pycnanthemum incanum. The hoariness of the leaves would seem to leave very little doubt and if there be any it will be removed by examining whether the stamens are exserted which I think is pretty clear and then distinguishing from aristatum by Michaux's figures.

Oct 17. Wednesday, Morning went down the Raleigh road and over to Scotts hole in search of a species of Gerardia which I did not find. Found however a species of Gentiana. Collected some Solidagos, Andropogons and Asters to send to Mr. Schweinitz.

Gentiana saponaria Elliott. Agrees perfectly with the description. Distinguished from Nos. 2.3 by the ovate segments of the calyx from Nos. 4.6.7 by leaves not linear nor amplexicaule and from No. 5. by the unfringed [?] corolla.

Nov 8. Since my last note have not been entirely inattentive to botany, and have in particular of late been attempting the mosses though the badness of my glasses hardly warrants the attempt. Got Bridels and my plants from Mr. Schweinitz to day I have ascertained as I hope 5 species of moss which I now set down merely to determine fully at some other time.

Polytrichum perigoniale. On the ivy hill above Kittrells. The fructification is just now making its appearance.

Polytrichum undulatum. Capsules of a mahogany colour now getting ripe.

[185]   Bartramia pomiformis. Capsule very round.

Hypnum minutulum. Pinnately branched – leaves very small to be much farther examined. Capsules getting ripe.

Hypnum riparioides. The season of fruit does not agree. Capsules getting ripe.

1822

[151]   **Feb 17, 1822**[!] Iterum "χαιρετε." Took a walk this morning down to Kittrells creek and was agreably surprised at finding that though I have suffered

the time to slip away till it is 12 days later than when I began the botanical campaign last year I am still in season. Alnus serrulata though near its time cannot be said to shed its pollen when struck with the finger.

Feb 22. Within 5 days Alnus serrulata nearly gone out of flower and Ulmus americanus is in full flower though the anthers are not yet burst.

Feb 22. Down about Scotts hole – ascertained the shrub in the pond to be Laurus geniculata of Pursh and Elliott. Corylus americana in flower – female [152] flowers above the male – red – male longer than those of Alnus serrulata.

Mar 1. Rambled out to the steep rocks south of Major Hendersons plantation where on a warm rock I found Erithronium lanceolatum and Hepatica triloba in full flower – Saxifraga virginiensis opening and Draba hispidula in the field–

Mar 4. Saw Houstonia caerulea and Draba verna in flower.

Mar 6. Some flowers of the red plum fully open.

Mar 9. No peach blossoms fairly open.

[105] Muscologia

Mar 9, 1822 [!] I to day make the first note on mosses.

Grimmia controversa. The first moss taken up by me. Agrees well with Smith and Bridel – The capsules are now ripe – the capsules of another moss growing with it are coming on – I should have no doubt did I not see Grimmia apicola put down in the N.Y. catalogue as flowering in April and May. [The "N.Y. catalogue" is perhaps Torrey, 1819.]

[152] **Apr 13.** Down toward Barbees on Bollings Creek. Found ["Arabis" crossed out] Arabis rhomboidea in flower in a branch and a plant believed Panax trifolium but I am not absolutely certain. The fruit to be watched for.

Barbarea vulgaris Nuttall or Erysimum barbarea which is frequently wild but I believe introduced about here ascertained by me.

Apr 17. To the ["corner" crossed out] bend in Morgan's creek at the Maples.

Viola concolor. A plant of which I could make nothing last year grows there plentifully. Did not find the yellow violet. Uvularia perfoliata I am right in by reason of the description in general and the acuminate leaves. See Bot. Ellisia nyctelea grows plentifully by the side of a rock in the field about half a mile above this and is in flower. Flowers white?

Apr 20. Down in Taylor's meadow east from the hill a plant in the old field is to be watched. Also a large plant. Diadelphia.

Thaspium barbinode. Which I have not been certain did not belong to Smyrnium aureum ascertained beyond all doubt from Nutall – description perfect except that the leaves of the involucele are lanceolate and the stem hardly angular. This whole family of umbellate plants must be reviewed. N. side of hill.

Orobanche uniflora. Found as I was passing through the woods. 23 again.

Apr 23. Down Bolling's Creek to Old Mr. Barbees.

Scirpus capitatus Elliott. Common in all wet places. Agrees well with Elliott. *Stem deeply sulcate. One sheath 1–2 inches long around the base* sometimes [illegible] very thin 5 to 10 inches high. Capitate. Scales ovate. Chocolate colour with [153] membranaceous margins. Very little doubt.

Carex multiflora. In my garden.

Triosteum angustifolium. Found a single root in the woods by the creek side. Agrees well.

Potamogeton [blank]. Leaves large in a small pond by the creek side.

Bletia aphylla. I have found this before on the 1 April beside Haw River near the ferry to Col. Jones' – I have little doubt.

Poa viridis. No doubt. The reddened extremities of the valves. Tomentum an decisivo and the leaf abruptly acuminate like the autumnalis. Notandum.

Gratiola sphaerocarpa. No doubt yet Elliott has represented the leaves as more obovate than they are. They are rather lanceolate. There is a Carex in Taylors meadow sometime gone to seed. N[ext] Year.

[149]   **Apr 26. 1822** [!] Panicum. The first in flower – Buds have come out but tis not yet open. Paniculate – therefore after 14. Nos. 18.19. not to be looked for here. Nor 37 at this season. Not 16.20.*21*. /flowers not large/.22 25.26 by reason of their height. 2. 2–3, 2. 2–2 1/2. 2–4. 2. feet. ["Nor 18" crossed out] Not 24 not "pubescent hoary sheaths very hairy or woolly at or near the throat." Not 28. not leaves linear lanceolate nor of a pale delicate green colour. (*Not 33 from its habitat*). (*Not 35. leaves not linear lanceolate.*) (*Not 36. leaves not long.*) (*Not 38 "1–3 feet high linear lanceolate"*). Not 39 leaves not subulate. There remain Nos 15.17.23.29.30.31.32 34 35. – Not 15. leaves not 1–1 1/2 inches wide. Not 17. not narrow lanceolate /nor flowers very large/ nor disposed to branch at the joints. Not 23. from its height 1–2 feet. and habitat Georgia Not 34. panicle not capillary leaves linear lanceolate. nor flowers minute – Not 35. leaves not linear lanceolate. Not 27. not (villous). Not 29. not hairy nor pale green. Not 30: panicle not "large." Not 34. not "large leaves to the base of the panicle" – There remain. 23.31.32.33.35. No 23 is thrown out by its height 1–2 feet. pubescent crowded leaves. Not 31. leaves not pale green. Not 35. not linear "lanceolate leaved flowers minute – leaves serrulate. joints beardless" There remain 31" 32. The acuminate leaves seem to point to "Ensifolium."

[111]   **May 6, 1822** [!] On the Carexes.

Carex festucacea. The plant I have must of course lie between Nos. 15 and 22 inclusive. The number of spiculae which in 16 specimens are on 9 – 5. on 5 – 6 and on 2 – 8. excludes at once Nos. 15.16.19. and the want of "bracteae foliaceae longissimae" excludes No. 21. There remains Nos. 17.18.20.22. Nos. 18. 20 are at first to be suspected – from the number of Spiculae "*Spiculis subsenis*" 2. from the habitat "New York" 20 is thrown out by Muhlenburg who describes it as having only the terminal spicules "basi Mascula" also Caps ovata *integra*. Festucacea agrees pretty well with Pursh. It does not agree well with Muhlenburg – Description 10 to 18 inches high when in seed – culm has two or three leaves – linear, extending to the height of 5 or 6 inches; the rest is bare – nearly round – striate where the leaves cease – becoming triquetrous at top. Spiculae alternate clavate obtuse – Female scale [illegible word crossed out] lanceolate membranous with a green keel about tho hardly as long as the capsule, mucronate – Capsule lenticular bicuspidate ciliate serrate especially near the apex. In my garden. April. I think I have the Festucacea at least of Pursh.

1823

[110]   **Feb 21, 1823** [!] The Alnus serrulata at Kittrells ford scantly sheds its pollen. I believe however that the buds have been injured by the frost. Caught an Acarus americanus [a wood tick] on the twenty-second.

Feb 22. Alnus in full flower in warm exposures.

Feb 23. Draba verna has been in flower two or three days as it has capsules. Saxifraga and Erythronium not yet out.

Mar 2. Erithronium and Saxifraga flowers opening on the warm rocks. South of Maj. Hendersons plantation Ulmus americanus and Acer rubrum just come in flower.

Mar 4. Cardamine virginica is just in flower on Sol. Morgans land.

Mar 23. To the laurel hill. The small Salix growing about here is just in flower and ["tho" crossed out] as I am far from certain about it I describe the flower and wait for the leaves. Male ament between ovate and cylindric – scale rather obovate acutish white at bottom then a small zone reddish top dark mahogany if not black and with long villosity springing at least from all the black part but most abundant at the edge so as to make the scale ciliate. Stamina white – Anthers dark red or purple before bursting – yellow after – Diandrous. Female ament as the other. Stigmas two bifid – red tomentose – Scale as before.

Apr 14. Scots Hole. Carex near the willows to be watched. [illegible]. Crataegus.

1824

[12]   Muscological Studies

[**Apr 24**]. I commence here my new diary of mosses with one I have this day ascertained, pretty much to my satisfaction. April 24, 1824 [!]. Leskea, Hypnum, Mnium and Bryum are all very nearly related. The number of exteriour teeth is the same in all – 16. The inner peristome in all is a delicate membrane ending variously. In Leskea in uniform acuminated teeth – in Hypnum in the same with intermediate fine ciliae – in these two the peduncles are always axillary. Mnium and Bryum are most closely related to Hypnum. Bryum differs *only* in the position of the peduncles and Mnium from Bryum in that the inner teeth are perforated. My glasses do not reach these generic distinctions and I must therefore be guided a good deal by the specific until Dr. Caldwell shall return [from Europe] with a good microscope.

Mnium cuspidatum. of Sprengel Bridel and Michaux. Bryum of Smith.

[188]   More Botany.

1824 [!] Christmas Day. Thlaspi bursa pastoris has been flowering ever since last spring. Found Draba verna and hispidula in flower.

Jan 16 [1825]. Draba verna and hispidula whiten the ground. Viola tricolor in flower. Alnus and Corylus do not seem to feel the influence of spring.

1825

[186]   **April 5, 1815** [!] I now take up my botanical studies for the first time this year and examine some plants collected on the first day of the month.

[The date 1815 was certainly a slip of the pen, for in that year Mitchell was still in New England. If we assume that the account of the three species that immediately follows was written at this time, we can feel some confidence that the correct date must be 1821 or later. In the first paragraph of description Mitchell cited such botanical works as Pursh (published 1816), Bigelow's *Medical Botany* (1817–1821), Eaton (1817 or probably 1818), and Elliott (the pertinent pages late 1821). In writing of the *Ranunculus*, Mitchell said, "I have formerly called it the fascicularis, and now believe I am right." This may well refer to his note of April 15, 1820, when he collected what he supposed to be *R. fascicularis* in approximately the same locality. We have selected the date 1825 because it is the earliest possible one after 1820–1824, when he began his botanical season on dates already known, and because it only requires Mitchell to have made a mistake in writing one digit, not two.]

Ranunculus fascicularis. Collected on the hill side south of Barbees-Daniel house. A pretty forward specimen and some of the corollas are withering. Stem rather decumbent, 6–8 inches long, purplish towards the bottom, a little channeled with silvery appressed hairs. Lowest root leaves 2.4 inches hairy above and below. Three *lobed* – lobes crenate. Some are ternate – some ternate with the leaflets three lobed and some with the leaflets cut. the lobes and segments toothed. *Most of the leaves in my present specimens are ternate with the leaflets three lobed*, undique pilosis. Stem leaves at the foot of each flower stalk exhibiting a tendency to be ternate with the leaflets lanceolate and simple. Flowers not numerous. Calyx expanding, very hairy. Corolla bright shining yellow obovate not emarginate, nearly twice the length of the calyx. Scale approaching to triangular /tis trapezoidal/ with the base uppermost. Stamina about 50. or 60. Seeds smooth beaked. Petals 5–8. Root fascicled. Not abortivus or nitidus of Pursh because I know the abortivus. Not sceleratus fide Elliott and Encyclopaedia on account of the nectary and great number of stamens. Not 10. of Pursh from its habitat – nor 12 from its fibrous root ["and it" crossed out]. Not 19 from its small flower nor 22.23. There remains /Encyclopaedia/ 9.11.13.14.15.16.17.18.21. /22.46.51.54.59.63.65.66.68.69/. Not 9. fide Encyclopaedia on account of the scale. Not 11 fide Encyclopaedia on account of the ["small" crossed out] large petals and shaggy calyx. Not 13. fide Ency. aut hirsutus because it has no tubercles. Not 14. from the want of runners and of an obcordate scale Encyc. Not 15. which I shall see in flower late in June next. Fide Bigelow Med. Bot. Not 16. from the /large/ heart shaped quinquefid leaves and striated flower stalks of 16 ["and" crossed out] Not 17. fide Encyclop. Not 18 which has a smooth calyx. Not 20 from the globular fruit of 20. and its almost smooth calyx otherwise it agrees pretty well. Not 21. from the small pale yellow flowers of 21.

I have formerly called it the fascicularis and now believe I am right and that it is likewise the nitidus of Elliott which is rendered *very* probable by the *square scale* and *many filaments*. See Eaton's Manual and Florula Bostoniensis.

[187] **Apr 12.** A new field. I crossed Bollings creek at the sawmill and passed up the branch to Lees – then down the creek [Presswood, now Booker, Creek] to Bevils and home. On the branch saw I believe a Corrallorhiza which is to be watched and some cresses which may turn out to be Cardamine pennsylvanica. Saw Arctium lappa ["and" crossed out] Neottia pubescens near the basin and Leonurus cardiaca by the side of Mr. Olmsted's house.

Corydalis aurea. Was found on the rocks overhanging the basin.

Melica glabra. The only thing which has puzzled me about this heretofore is the part which says that the neutral floret is between the others. This I now understand as between the others means merely lying between them – higher on the rachis.

Carex miliacea. The description agrees well except the scale which I have not yet examined.

Carex hirsuta. Found near the spring below Barbees Daniel House. Agrees well with Muhlenberg [*sic*]. A foot to a foot and a half high. The base not nigrescent. Leaves linear lanceolate, slightly pubescent on the upper abundantly on the lower side. *Vagina pubescent*. Spikes generally 4. Spikes as discribed except that the lowest in these specimens is on a peduncle an inch long. Bractea as described and so of the rest. Capsule [?] larger than the scale. Hardly any room for doubt but I believe it varies a good deal.

[178]   [**May 23.**] Genus Panicum.

We have a number of species of the paniculate Panica "floribus diffusis solitariis" to which I seriously sit down May 23 1825 [!].

Panicum ciliatum. The earliest in the spring.

Panicum pubescens. ["of the delicate" crossed out] With the narrow leaves and largish fruit.

Panicum strigosum. With delicate green leaves.

Panicum villosum. With leaves soft like velvet. From 1 1/2 to 2 1/2 feet high, with axillary branches after the first flowering. Stem smooth. Nodes hairy. Sheaths pubescent, much shorter than the joints. Leaves lanceolate from 2 to 4 inches long, from 4 to 8 lines wide. Stipules inconspicuous. Has the softest leaves of any plant I know, occasioned by a fine short villosity. Panicle 2 to 4 inches long expanding. In common with the rest of the plant has a reddish cast. Flowers numerous small, ovate cov. with white hairs.

Panicum latifolium. [name only]

[179] Panicum pauciflorum. Very large fruit and broadish lanceolate leaves. Flowering May 23. Averaging about 12 inches erect columnar. Stem and sheaths hairy somewhat hoary, leaves about 3 inches long, 1/2 an inch wide, smooth above roughish below – remarkable for the ciliate stipules: ciliae a quarter of an inch long. Fruit obovate. Accessory /valve/ 1/4 or 1/3 the other. Fruit 20 or 30.

Panicum [blank]. Nearly related to the preceding.

Panicum nitidum. In my garden.

Panicum. [name only]

[In the above list the epithets *strigosum*, *villosum*, *latifolium*, *pauciflorum*, and *nitidum* have been added in pencil, as if representing tentative determinations after the original list was drawn up; *pauciflorum* has then been inked in.]

1828

[100] [Apparently in April or May, 1828, Mitchell applied himself for a time to the genus *Carex*, which had always interested him and to an extent puzzled and frustrated him, and compiled a list of local species, numbered from 1 to 21.]

Carexes

1. Carex varia. Laurel Hill on the rock with the Mitchella repens. Collected fine specimens in seed April 18th 1828 [!]. Grows here in tufts – and the specimens are large and flourishing. Culm 10.12 inches high, ["leafy" crossed out] obscurely triquetrous, smooth except just at the top, leafy at the base to the height of one or two inches only. Leaves – 1–3 inches long, linear scabrous on the margin, but some of the leaves that come out /during the summer/ upon stems that are to produce next year are 12 inches long. Male spike, terminal, sessile, cylindrical about half an inch long – a little more. Glumes – reddish brown with a white margin – Female spikes 2–4, sessile, the lowest commonly with *a linear leafy bractea sometimes an inch in length.* Spikes from 5 to 10 flowered, Fruit triquetrous, pubescent on a pretty long stem, attenuate towards both extremities (clavate). Scale, suddenly a little mucronate – whitish /sometimes brown/ with a green keel. not quite as long as the fruit.

Specimens from the woods about Chapel Hill differ as follows [paragraph ends, but a space of five lines has been left]. [Mitchell returned to this plant a few pages later.]

[107]   Carex varia [these words were subsequently crossed out] (Muhlenburg). The Carex growing on the rocks of Laurel Hill is either *varia or marginata. I take it to be varia for the following reasons.* [ends].

[100]   2. Carex conoidea? Common in woods and thickets by the sides of fields in good arable land. In flower and fruit April 16th 1828. Grows in tufts. Stems 12 inches high, when tallest very weak and slender, obscurely triquetrous – smooth except just at the summit. Leaves 2–4 inches long, 1–1 1/2 lines broad – a little rough on the margin. Male spike on a peduncle 4 inches long proceeding from the same sheath with the upper female spike, inclosed by the whitish sheath to the distance of nearly an inch. Spike a little more than 1/2 an inch long cylindrical. Scale (when the fruit is mature) light brown, lanceolate, very obtuse, membranaceous with a green keel. Female spikes /3/, all long pedunculate upper 3. Second 4 1/2 Third 4 inches peduncles very slender sheathed about an inch at base, fruit nodding. Spikes 8.8. and 6 flowered, flowers loosely arranged. Fruit. ovate and triquetrous. Stigmas 3. One of the triquetrous sides (the inner) longer than the other two. Scales membranous, whitish keel green, sometimes acute but hardly mucronate – half the length of the fruit. Is either this or laxiflora.

[101]   I cannot but suspect that varia and marginata are the same. My specimens agree with varia in the sessile male spike, disagree in their bractea, but accord in this, and its pedicellate fruit with marginata.

3. Carex retroflexa. Grows in rather damp arable land. Flower and fruit April 16, 1828. In tufts. 8–15 inches high. Stem very slender, nearly round, leafy nearly half its height. root leaves sometimes as long as the stem; stem leaves shorter – 2–5 inches – not more than a line broad; scabrous on the margin. About half a dozen small spikes are tolerably distinct at first but more confluent after it, and the upper also more aggregated than the lower, supported by an awn contracted suddenly into a bristle – in the case of the lowest half an inch in length, in the others much shorter, deciduous. Summit staminiferous, Stigmas 2. Scale membranous with a green keel. rather acute. Fruit 2–6 to each spike, roundish yet flattened on the interior side acute, reflexed.

4. Carex anceps [name only; nine lines left blank for description]

5. Carex caespitosa. Mr Taylors field beyond Bolling creek in the swamp. [nine lines left blank on pp. 101–102 for description]

[102]   6. Carex acuta. In the swamp in the field of Mr. Taylor beyond Bollings creek. [nine lines left blank]

7. Carex digitalis? Mr. Barbees Daniel place in the field below the house near the branch. [eight lines left blank]

8. Carex festucacea. Solomon Morgan's field near Scotts hole. [eight lines left blank]

[103]   9. Carex hirsuta. Same field with the last. [eight lines left blank]

10. Carex multiflora [written over an illegible word?]. Same field with the last. [then, with a different pen] Also in Merits meadow abundantly. Stem 12. 18 inches high, nearly round at the base, leafy to near half its height. Leaves 6 inches to a foot long, 1–2 lines wide, caniculate very acute, scabrous on the midrib and margin – stipules rounded, entire, below them the sheath is membranaceous to some distance and wrinkled – stem above the leaves at first obscurely – afterwards decidedly triquetrous – spike 1–2 inches long rather cylindrical, supradicompound? With 5–6 spikelets branching /over/ into smaller spikelets – and a top consisting of unbranched spikelets sitting closely upon the rachis, each small spike androgynous – masculine at tops. Stigmas 2. Scale membraneous green on the keel, about as long as the fruit, ovate acute. Fruit, much compressed, broad ovate, acute, serrate on the margin.

11. Carex [blank]. Common in swampy meadows. Flowers about the middle of April at the same time with the preceding which in its general habit and manner of flowering it a good deal resembles. It grows in wetter ground, is more triquetrous, of a yellower green – that is dark green, and its fruit is quite different. Stem [ends; nine lines left blank]

[104]   12. Carex tentaculata. Grows abundantly about the head of Merrits Mill Pond. [ten lines left blank].

["13" has been omitted].

14. Carex crinita. Common by the side of streams. May. beginning. [eight lines left blank]

[105]   15. Carex folliculata. In Mr Kittrells field up toward McCauleys. [ten lines left blank]

16. Carex [blank]. Same field with the last near the slippery elm tree. Related to anceps and what is here called conoidea, differing in its awned scale especially. [twelve lines left blank]

[106]   17. Carex [blank]. Nearly related to festucacea. [ten lines left blank]

18. Carex squarrosa. [name only; ten lines left blank]

19. Carex miliacea.[name only; nine lines left blank]

[107]   20. Carex willdenowii? [name only; nine lines left blank, on the fifth of which "Carex conoidea" has been crossed out. Then, after a double line drawn across the page:]

Carex conoidea [these words have been crossed out]. An old enemy. Grows in wet ground at least generally. Stigmas two – spikes androgynous – masculine at the base. In the class between 15 and 22 of Pursh. 8. to which is to be added Straminea from Barton and Encyclopaedia. No. 17.21. are thrown out: "Bracteis foliaceis longissimis."– No. 15. "Spiculis tribus congestis" of Pursh and Ency. No. 16 by P and Muhlenburg "Foliis glaucis scabris – Spicis tribus – infima bracteata ceteris ebracteatis – Bractea spicula longiore" together with the remark. No. 18 by Smith "Culmus acute triqueter." "Bractea foliacea ad basin spiculae infimae" "Flores masculi pauci foeminei numerosi." – Straminea. "Spike compound – *spikelets* subglobose almost close together." Barton. Muhlenburg.

[Here a line has been drawn across the page.]

Improbable – No. 22 "Spikelets about 8, merely close together" – Barton – fruit larger than the scale. Yet it may be scoparia, festucacea, curta with which last canescens, elongata and loliacea are said to be the same. Ency. Descriptions Culm 10 to 18 inches – *Obscurely triquetrous* except toward the top – striate. Rough at the edges within 3 inches of the top. leafy from 1/3 to 1/2 its height. Leaves linear carinate rough at the edges only, not as long as the culm ligula membranaceous. Spikes 6. sometimes 5 or 7 – seldom 4 or 8. cylindrical, masculine below, the male part at first occupying two thirds of the spike, the spikes near yet perfectly distinct. A membranaceous – green – carinate awned bractea always appearing, 1/2 as long /including the awn/ as the spike in the lowest – diminishing so as almost to disappear above.

[108]   perhaps withering and deciduous – not pubescent but very smooth. Scale ovate membranaceous green, carinate, acute – Stamina 3, white. Capsule notandum. Against the three species between which it lies are the following characters. Muhlen.

Festucacea. Spike composite – spikelets 8 – Caps.

Curta. *Lower* spike with linear pubescent bractea – and the *terminal* masculine at the base – Caps. is if recollect right a good deal toothed

Scoparia. Spike composite. Spikelets 5. the lowest bracteated. Caps.

As Willldenow gives to scoparia a lanceolate mucronate bractea, a marginate ["and Muhlenberg" crossed out] capsule, I shall call it at present Carex scoparia. [The last two words have been crossed out, and Mitchell adds:] Is it not brizoides? cf Cyclopaedia.

[A second double line is here drawn across the page.]

21. Carex cephalophora? Pretty common in dryish ground. Flowers end of April. Stem 1–2 feet high, acutely triquetrous, smooth except on the edges near the top, leafy only near the base, leaves longer than the stem, 2 lines wide. smooth except on the edges. tapering very gradually till they become filiform and setaceous. Spike consisting of one principal terminal spikelet with three others attached to the stem *at* its base so that the four form one compact head. Spikelets androgynous. stameniferous at the summit. Female portion when the fruit approaches to maturity squarrose, densely fruited, scale small ovate, membranaceous, with a setaceous awn 2 or three times its length equalling /if not exceeding/ in length the fruit. Fruit ovate [illegible] compressed (meniscate) with an involute beak. very slightly if at all serrate. The fruit resembles somewhat that of multiflora but it is more compressed, has a longer beak and the scale is altogether different.

[We find no evidence in Mitchell's notes that he involved himself with *Carex* after his flurry of interest in 1828, but it is at least suggestive that M. A. Curtis dedicated to him a new species, *Carex mitchelliana*. The plant was said to have been found in 1835, in wet places in Chatham County, North Carolina (Curtis 1843, p. 84). Mitchell was not named as the collector of the plant, and no specific locality in Chatham County was named, but as the northern part of the county was well within Mitchell's botanizing range, it is quite possible that he did indeed discover the plant and refer it to Curtis. On the other hand, Chester Dewey (Dewey, 1845) said of the plant, "discovered by the Rev. Moses A. Curtis, in wet places in Chatham County"; did Dewey have independent knowledge of the discovery, or was he inferring from Curtis's description that Curtis himself had discovered it? Unfortunately, type specimens of the species have not been located by subsequent researchers, as we were kindly informed by Leo P. Bruederle (letter, June 10, 1995). In any case, Mitchell's interest in botany did continue into the year 1835 and beyond, as the following entries show.]

1835

[18] **Sept. 19th, 1835** [!] Engaged once more in botany. Examined a pea with a purple flower very common in the fields.

Phaseolus helvolus of Michaux, probably also of Pursh, allowing an error in his description "*alis expansis maximis*" which plant appears never to have been seen except by himself. I have unquestionably the Strophostyles peduncularis of Elliott but not probably the vexillatus of Pursh /as Elliott supposes/ unless his vexillatus and helvolus be a species and and an accidental variety. The vexillatus of Sir E. Smith (Rees) appears to be different certainly and probably different from any species in the United States. The generic distinctions of Phaseolus and Dolichos to be examined. Peduncularis probably a better name for this species than helvolus though the latter – "pale red" agrees well – /In dry fields/ Very com[mon].

Aster patens of Pursh examined. See the pages on the Asters (common dry woods).

Prenanthes. [name only; four lines left blank]

Sep 21. Verbesina coreopsis of Pursh. Actinomeris squarrosa of Elliott. Description agrees /with Elliott/ except that the leaves of the involucrum are in a double series! or rather I have taken the outer chaff for leaves of the involucrum. Florets of the ray in one instance six, lanceolate not *linear* lanceolate, and the seed very decidedly winged.

Liatris macrostachya? Two to three feet high. Leaves, lower sometimes. 6 or 7 inches long not above a quarter of an inch wide in the widest part. They dwindle upwards to less than an inch in length and are subulate, Stem /at bottom/ and upper side of the large leaves hairy /or villous/. Leaves have straggling ciliae along their edges /throughout their lower half/. Flowers sometimes 28 in number, nearly sessile /with [illegible] bractea/ ["rather sessile" crossed out]. Florets from 6 to 10 – /Calyx cylindrical/. Involucrum imbricate lanceolate or ligulate, scariose and fringed on the edges, upper members coloured at the extremity, not mucronate, appressed. Florets when fully expanded twice or more the length of the calyx. Papus feathered, coloured, about as long as the seed, common. Not pycnostachya "calycibus superne squarrosis" graminifolia "floribus remotiusculis
[19]   calycinis squamis mucronatis" heterophylla, aspera "lanceolate leaves" – cylindracea "spica rariflora squamis calycinis mucronatis" – pilosa no very good reason – gracilis, calycibus subglobosis – elegans no good reason – sphaeroidea, scariosa the leaves – squarrosa the calyx. May be macrostachya, graminifolia? pilosa, elegans. Pursh May be macrostachya, graminifolia? Elliott. Not pilosa E. "peduncles one half to one inch long" "corolla scarcely longer than the involucrum" "pappus not coloured" – gracilis "Peduncles nearly an inch long furnished with a few small scales" – secunda flowers secund on peduncles from half an inch to an inch long – resinosa heads resinous 4–5 flowered – elegans leaves linear *lanceolate*. The great objection to macrostachya is the width of the leaves. Judging from the leaves *alone* it should be pycnostachya tenuifolia cylindracea pilosa gracilis secunda. Resinosa!

[Sep?] 24. Prenanthes alba. Flowers yellowish white, involucrum 8 leaved, 9.10 flowered. Grows in Mr Whytes field where were several stems differing *widely* from each other in the shape of the leaves. The *number* of the flowers and divisions of the calyx excludes the juncea, altissima and cordata. The stem not "simplicissimus" colour of the corolla virgata and simplex. The number of the florets in excess – Crepidisa [= *crepidinea*]. Leaves not entire Rubicunda. The habitat and other characters. Nos. 10.11. It may agree better with Serpentaria. Dried top and large leaves from one stem, piece of stem from two others. *We have another species.* Nutall says alba and serpentaria are hardly distinct. The colour of the flowers agrees with alba and the size better than with serpentaria.

Liatris scariosa and squarrosa. The scariosa in my field in the moist untilled new ground and the squarrosa near the big rock.

1837

[188]   **May 3d, 1837** [!]. Phlox setacea. I have wavered betwixt setacea and subulata and now call it setacea on the score of the calyx which in the subulata are a little shorter or about as long as the tube of the corolla. Torrey. Beck. but in the setacea much shorter (Torrey) triplo brevioribus – Pursh. The stem is hairy and the calyx hardly half as long as the tube of the corollas. The other characters agree best with subulata and I believe Elliott calls that I now have subulata.

Ranunculus fascicularis. Lowest leaves hairy or hairy petioles. Trifid deeply, the segments rounded toothed, newer ["higher" crossed out] leaves ternate, folioles deeply trifid and toothed. Stem leaves also ternate with toothed folioles. About a foot high, hair not appressed. Flowers large as R. bulbosus. Calyx hairy not reflexed, corolla petals twice the length of the sepals of the calyx with a cuneiform scale. Caryopsis beaked smooth head round.

[135] [**Jul 7**]. Monarda mollis. Collected July 7th 1837 [!] in the ascent of the hill to Mr. Potts's. Torrey is the best authority. The "*galea apice longissime barbata*" is a wart on a man's nose. My specimen is nearly smooth, a little downy about the joints and on the leaves, stalk obtusely angled, leaves petioled, serrated, coming down obtusely to the petiole. bracteas, slightly coloured on the inside, *ovate-lanceolate* calyx. fauce barbata, corolla flesh-coloured – pubescent.

APPENDIX A
CHAPEL HILL'S TOPOGRAPHY AND MITCHELL'S BOTANIZING LOCALITIES

The University of North Carolina began operation in 1795, upon a large tract of land that had been donated (except for one parcel of 80 acres that was purchased in 1793) by public-spirited citizens. The university lands were concentrated on and around the summit of a prominent hill at the crossing of two old trade routes, the one from Petersburg (Virginia) southwesterly toward the headwaters of the Cape Fear River, the other from Wilmington and Fayetteville northwesterly toward what is now Greensboro. The chapel for which the hill was named was more or less in ruins, but had formerly stood near the junction of the two roads, apparently in the vicinity of the present Carolina Inn. Except for these roads the hill was mostly forested and virtually unpopulated.

The University's property rights once established, its trustees planned for a village within their boundaries and auctioned off lots — mostly of two acres, but a few of four — along three streets: Main Street (called Franklin Street by at least 1806); Back Street (later to become Rosemary Street), parallel to it; and, at right angles to the first two, Columbia (at first known as "Fayetteville") Street. Franklin Street and Back Street were laid out to run more or less ENE – WSW, or more precisely N 62° E – S 62° W. The lots were assigned numbers by which they continued to be identified as they changed hands during the decades that followed, and this makes it possible to trace their history through the deeds recorded in the Orange County offices in Hillsborough (the individual lots are discussed in detail in Appendix E). Although a lively land market soon sprang up, it is clear that many of these lots were not immediately developed and long remained merely woodlots, pastures, or farmland. In January 1818, when Mitchell arrived, the village consisted merely of a dozen or so shops and dwellings strung out along the north and west sides of "the buildings of the university," which at that time numbered only three.

William D. Moseley graduated in that same year of 1818, and thirty-five years later he wrote to Mitchell to reminisce about the Chapel Hill he remembered:

> I would like…to take a stroll through the village; beginning at Mrs. Nunn's, and going eastwardly down the main Street, first by Mrs Mitchell's on the right; Trice's store on the left; Then Major Hendersons, Then James Hogg's immediately opposite; then the tavern occupied by Hilliard; Then Tom Taylors store, on the left, Then Edmund Pitts dwelling, then

Tom Taylors, Then (East of the Raleigh road), Dr. Caldwells residence, Then Mr Hooper's; immediately opposite to the latter was Mrs Puckets – This was then the principal Street; South from Mrs Nunn's was Wm Barbee's, Then the President's house, occupied by yourself. Then, So West, Mrs. Pannill's and Watson's – These I believe, were at the time the houses composing the village; with two college buildings; and Person Hall – Chapel.[1]

Moseley's memory was generally good, even if his topography is a little unclear, as can be seen by reference to Map 2. That map and its explanatory text, and the statements in the rest of this and the next few paragraphs, are mostly from the county records in Hillsborough; they do not always agree with Battle (1907, 1912) or with Henderson (1949). Mrs. Elizabeth Nunn kept a boarding-house at the southwestern corner of Franklin and Columbia Streets on lot 5; her son David owned until 1809 the western half of lot 6, across Columbia Street. Farther east, on lot 9, the widow Sarah Mitchell (no relation to Elisha) took in boarders, and then, on lot 11, James Hogg lived in a "store house" at the edge of the "Grand Avenue" (a broad strip of land running north parallel to Columbia Street, originally planned as a formal opening preserved for its future aesthetic value but later reduced in width to become modern Henderson Street, with the remainder sold off for development). Across Franklin Street, northeast of the corner of Franklin and Columbia Streets, lot 8 had been subdivided and held Christopher Barbee's blacksmith shop and a "storehouse" built by George Trice. Next to it, lot 10 had also been split in half: the western half was owned by Major Pleasant Henderson until April 1822, when he sold it to Benjamin Rhodes, and the eastern half was owned by Edmund Pitt until he sold it to John Ramsey in 1821 (Rhodes would acquire this half, too, in 1824). The last lot (12) on the north side of Franklin Street, just west of the Grand Avenue, held Major Henderson's residence.

Across the Grand Avenue to the east from Major Henderson's home, a "shoe shop" owned by merchant Thomas Taylor in the 1810s and 1820s was on the western half of lot 14, whose eastern half Edmund Pitt had bought in 1813; next on the east, William and Harrison Trice owned lot 16 from 1819 to 1827. Finally, on the north side of Franklin Street at its corner with the road running to Hillsborough (i.e., the northern continuation of the "Raleigh road" referred to by Moseley), John Taylor, the first Steward of the University, owned lot 18; he also owned lots 15 and (after 1796) 13, across Franklin Street. In 1818 lot 13 held Hilliard's Hotel (later the Eagle Hotel), but lots 15 and 18 were undeveloped; John Taylor sold them both to his son Thomas in December 1824. Thomas Taylor had already bought lot 17 (in 1814) and was living there in a house he had built.

East of the Hillsborough road there was apparently only one house on the north side of Franklin Street. Dr. Elias Hawes had bought lot 20 in 1809, but he built nothing on the property and sold it in 1831 to James Phillips, Professor of Mathematics at the University. The eastern half of lot 22 was undeveloped; the western half was bought in 1817 by Jane Puckett, the widow of a former postmaster; she built a house on the lot and sold the property in 1820 to Mitchell's colleague, Denison Olmsted. Olmsted found the expense of enlarging and renovating the Puckett house enough of a burden that he arranged for the trustees to

---

[1]Based on Henderson (1949), p. 56. We have incorporated minor corrections from the original letter, William D. Moseley to Elisha Mitchell, Aug. 13, 1853, in University papers, UNC-CH Library.

buy it from him in 1822, though he continued to live there at least for a time (he resigned to return to Yale in 1825).[2]

Lot 24, the last on the north side of Franklin Street, "the most easterly lot in the plan of the village," was unused, though John Caldwell, who had bought it from the trustees in 1793, had lived on the eastern half before giving it up in a sheriff's sale in 1815. On the south side of this part of Franklin Street there were but two houses. President Caldwell had acquired all three of the lots (19, 21, and 23) between the Hillsborough–Raleigh road and the end of the village (modern Boundary Street), but in May 1819 he divided the property roughly in half and sold the eastern half (parts of lots 21 and 23) to his stepson William Hooper, Professor of Ancient Languages at the University. South of Hooper's house, on a larger, four-acre lot (lot VI), was a house that Moseley did not mention: it had been the home of Abner Clopton, the last headmaster of the university's short-lived preparatory school, but Hooper had bought it from Clopton at the same time he bought the property on Franklin Street from Caldwell. From the existing house Hooper no doubt kept an eye on the house he proceeded to build on the lot next to his stepfather, and once the house was finished he sold lot VI and its house to Shepard Kollock, Professor of Rhetoric from 1819 to 1825. Hooper had for the moment a short tenure in the new house, as he resigned from the university and left Chapel Hill at the end of the 1821–1822 school year, but he returned in 1828 to teach again.

The remainder of the houses in the village were on Columbia Street. Except for lot 5 already mentioned, the west side (lots 1, 3, 7) was apparently still undeveloped in 1818. On the east side lot 4, owned by William Barbee, was also undeveloped, though Moseley seems to imply that Barbee, at that time Steward and Superintendent of the University, lived there. Lot 2 was university property, the "president's lot," where Elisha Mitchell (and, after her arrival in 1819, his wife) shared the house (built in 1795 and originally intended for the president) with Olmsted until the latter bought the Puckett house; President Caldwell had chosen to live farther away from the students, on Franklin Street. Finally, farther south of lots 1 and 2, across an "avenue" (now Cameron Avenue), were two of the six four-acre lots sold by the trustees. William Pannill had bought lot II and a half of lot I in 1817, and lived there, taking in students as boarders — as did most of the residents of the village. The other half of lot I was bought by Mitchell in 1819, just after he returned from the North with a bride, perhaps with the expectation of living there one day, but in fact the Mitchells never moved out of "the president's house" north of "the avenue." That house was more or less where modern Swain Hall now stands, about one hundred meters from Columbia Street, and perhaps twice as far from Moseley's "two college buildings; and Person Hall–Chapel" — which is to say, the East Building (dating from 1793), the Main [South] Building (1798–1814), and the east wing of Person Hall, the old Chapel (1797).

It would have been natural if in Mitchell's first season of botanizing (1819) he had begun by familiarizing himself with the plants in the village. One of the four

---

[2]There has been some debate over the age of the so-called Widow Puckett house, now a Chapel Hill landmark. Since Olmsted complained to the trustees of the costs of rebuilding it (letters of Dec. 14, 1821; Mar. 4, Aug. 10, and Sep. 19, 1822; in University papers, UNC-CH Library), it must have been on the site at that time. While the lot on which it stands was sold to "Jane" Puckett only in 1817 (see village lot 22, below), Henderson (1949, p. 57) says, "Mrs. Elizabeth [sic] Puckett's house . . . is said, on doubtful authority, to have been built prior to 1796. She was certainly taking students as boarders in 1796."

identifications he recorded from that year is of what he called an *Antirrhinum* collected "between my house and the college." But certainly from 1820 on he found it more profitable to do his botanizing in the fields and in the forested creek valleys that flanked "the hill." Nevertheless, he remained well aware of the common plants that grew in the village and took note of unusual species that he chanced upon there, like the yucca he found growing (presumably cultivated) in Mrs. Caldwell's yard on Franklin Street, or the *Leonurus* he saw across the street, "by the side of Mr. Olmsted's house." The space between the buildings of the college and Franklin Street, then called the Grove, had not been cleared and remained heavily wooded. In 1821 Mitchell made note of the half-dozen species of oaks he found there, including what he called *Quercus obtusifolia*, or post oak. Four years later (Henderson, 1949, p. 60) he observed with regret that "the oak trees in the Campus were failing, and that there was no undergrowth from which a supply of new trees was obtainable," but it seems that some of these oaks still survive. Every day, on his walk from his house to the college or chapel, Mitchell must have passed the then-young post oak that at one time in the late 1980s was accounted the national champion of its species (by a point rating calculated by adding the girth of the trunk, the total height, and one fourth of the spread of the crown). The tree still stands back of Old West, but it has since lost its championship standing to an even larger tree in Virginia.

Aside from the village, when Mitchell wanted to do serious botanizing he walked down the hill to one creek or the other. Chapel Hill is well named. On all sides of the village except from the west the only approaches are by fairly long, steep hills. The university and the village that was originally founded on university land lie on a high ridge between two deep creek valleys, Bolin's Creek to the north and Morgan's Creek to the south, both flowing generally easterly. In Mitchell's time (as at present), to gain access to Bolin's Creek (he usually spelled it "Bowlings" or "Bollings") one route was directly north, down a steep hill that was in his time still being cleared of trees. In one of his notes he said, "by the side of the near road to Hillsborough north of the village in the descent of the hill"; the other road to Hillsborough went farther to the northeast, more or less along the "Great Road" to Petersburg, to approach Hillsborough by way of New Hope. Close to where the "near road" crossed the creek (east of present Airport Road) was a grist mill on the south bank. On the steep hillside in the village and below it were a number of springs draining into Bolin's Creek. The Preparatory School set up in 1795 to bring prospective students up to University level had been placed in the Grand Avenue, north of Franklin Street, "in the woods, in a lonely spot, but with two unfailing springs" (Battle, 1907, p. 65). The "lonely spot" was between Rosemary and Franklin Streets, today in the midst of downtown Chapel Hill. After Abner Clopton resigned as headmaster of the Preparatory School in 1819, the year Mitchell began serious botanizing, the school building was occupied for a time by a professional hunter and his family, which suggests that game still roved in some quantities in the nearby forests.

Mitchell's notes show that he botanized on several occasions below the village on this side: "sides of the small streams north of the village"; "Mr. Taylors field below the Prep School"; "in the same field on the lately cleared side hill"; "same field by the brook"; "on the bank below the preparatory school." The steep slopes and springy ground have slowed development on this side of Chapel Hill, so that even today no street north of Rosemary (the "Back Street" of the two original streets) is cut through all the way from east to west.

A second and somewhat less abrupt access to Bolin's Creek lay to the east and northeast of the village. This would have been the route that Mitchell walked when he went "in a southeasterly direction on Bollings Creek" or "down toward Barbees on Bollings Creek." Before Mitchell's time, and before the streets of the village were laid out in squares, the old trade route from Petersburg, Virginia, crossed the Chapel Hill in a southwesterly direction; this was one of the "Great Roads" that are often mentioned on land-deeds as late as 1820. For example, the boundary between the tract donated to the trustees in 1796 by Benjamin Yeargain and the tract purchased by the trustees from Hardy Morgan in 1793 followed the Great Road to Petersburg from near the center of the modern campus (not far from the Old Well) approximately as far as present Rosemary Street, which it intersected near the present corner of Rosemary and Glenburnie. The descent beyond that point being too steep for most vehicles, the road was diverted to the right at an early date (apparently before John Daniel's survey of 1792 was completed), so as to follow more or less the course of modern Franklin Street, crossing the creek at the bottom of the hill. Mitchell noted once, the date uncertain but perhaps in 1825 (see page 57), "A new field, I crossed Bollings Creek at the sawmill [not far above where present Franklin Street crosses the creek] and passed up the branch [Schoolhouse Branch, now dry but then running southeasterly into Bolin's Creek near the sawmill] to Lees — then down the creek to Bevils and home." This one trip via the properties of "Lee" (James B. Leigh) and Bevill would have taken him into another watershed, that of Booker Creek (then usually called Presswood Creek). In the 1820s Booker Creek was far out in the country; it is now almost swallowed up in suburban Chapel Hill, piped and carried under a shopping mall (Eastgate) about three miles from the town center.

Although Mitchell's notes show that he botanized on more than a few occasions below the village in the valley of Bolin Creek (as it is officially known today), he spent considerably more time in the somewhat more precipitous valley to the south, that of Morgan Creek, where there were three large mills within walking distance: Barbee's mill farthest downstream, at the edge of the present lands of the North Carolina Botanical Garden; then Merritt's mill, near the road to Pittsboro; and McCauley's mill, somewhat farther upstream. When Mitchell notes that he went "down the creek," or "down to the creek," he usually means Morgan Creek, via the Pittsboro road, though this may not always be so. When he mentions "The Hill" he means the high ridge between the creeks, where the village and the university stood, and stand.

One of the steepest and most scenic parts of the valley of Morgan Creek extends down the creek southeasterly for a little more than two miles from where the Chapel Hill–Pittsboro road crosses it near the former site of Merritt's mill, and this was one of Mitchell's favorite areas, which he mentioned in his notes at least thirty-five times (he almost invariably used the spelling "Merit"). Merritt's meadow, a popular botanizing spot of his on the north side of the creek just below the mill, supported some wetland species. The meadow is still recognizable as such, though somewhat overgrown, and long in use as a pasture.

Upstream from and adjoining Merritt's land, and above the Pittsboro road, which has been scarcely relocated since Mitchell's time, was the property of Bryant Kittrell, through which Morgan Creek passed for some distance, perhaps a mile. This was another of Mitchell's favorite botanizing areas: his notes include at least thirty references to Mr. Kittrell's creek, his ford, his fish traps in the creek, and his spring.

On the other side of Merritt's property (downstream), Mitchell found it easy to go down the creek in the direction of Barbee's mill, the foundations of which are still visible. The mill was on the south side of Morgan Creek near the point where it emerges from the steepest part of the valley, just west of where the creek makes a sharp bend to the left, a few hundred meters above the municipal sewage treatment plant. The site is now on the lands of the North Carolina Botanical Garden, and has been somewhat protected from development. Mitchell's notes show that he often walked along the creek, both above and below the mill, or sometimes rode horseback or in a carriage: "ride down to Barbees mill and the creek below"; "road by Barbees plantation this side of his mill"; "down the creek opposite Barbees plantation"; "down the creek about Barbees mill"; "below Barbees mill"; "between Merit and Barbees mills"; "creek below Merits and the road toward Barbees mill"; "bank of the creek between Barbees and Merits mills, north side where a small branch runs down a ravine into it."

There were several attractive spots on the way down to and somewhat beyond Barbee's mill, some of which — especially Laurel Hill, Whetstone Rocks, and Scotts Hole — Mitchell visited more than once. Some of the area, now comprising part of the lands of the North Carolina Botanical Garden, has been protected from development; but for the most part, Mitchell's Chapel Hill, like a number of the plants he found there, is gone forever.

APPENDIX B
THE GENESIS OF MAP 1

A carefully formulated map can be a great aid in understanding historical geography. The original intent of the editors was to be able to visualize the village of Chapel Hill as it appeared to Elisha Mitchell, and thereby to retrace his botanizing expeditions upon today's landscape. The first draft of the map was a hand-drawn plot of the large tracts donated to the University at its beginning. This provided little information as to where Mitchell might have walked in relation to the environs of twentieth-century Chapel Hill. To tie old Chapel Hill to the present it was necessary to locate at least two specific landmarks that existed in Mitchell's day, and are still discernible today.

Mitchell often gave information in his notes about the locations, topography, and ownership of the tracts he explored. Of these characteristics, property boundaries are the easiest to recover with any degree of accuracy. Because of the special circumstances under which Chapel Hill was created, the first step was easily taken. For the most part, the parcels of land that were donated for the formation of the University adjoined one another, and together they comprised a large area that could be precisely located, once any two fixed points had been identified.

As it happens, the boundaries of some of those original tracts are still recognizable today. The boundary between the present-day neighborhood of Davie Circle and Battle Park, for example, was originally a part of the boundary of Hardy Morgan's property acquired by the University trustees (in consideration of a payment of five shillings) in 1796. North Carolina coordinates for the endpoints of that boundary line were scaled from the Orange County tax map of the area, and provided the starting points for our map. Using these coordinates and the line between them as a baseline, the grants to the University were plotted and overlaid on the USGS topographic map of the Chapel Hill Quadrangle (scale = 1 : 24000, 1978 edition).

In order to do this, however, it was necessary to correct for the change in magnetic declination over the last two hundred years. The bearing of the original line, obtained by inversing between the sets of scaled coordinates, gave a rough estimate of the approximate declination of magnetic north at the time of the original donations to the trustees of the University. Since magnetic north fluctuates east or west of true or astronomic north in a cycle of approximately 300 years, with small daily and annual variations, it was necessary to establish the angular difference between the magnetic bearings of the old deed descriptions and the grid north used on the USGS map, based on latitude and longitude. The bearings and distances for each grant were entered into a computer with a surveying software system, and the endpoints were plotted on a dot-matrix printer. The lines between the points were drawn on clear mylar film, and became the foundation of our Map 1.

The original deeds usually provided us with information on the ownership of the lands adjoining the lands that were donated, so that we were able to extend our map by by searching the indexes of the Register of Deeds at Hillsborough, the county seat of Orange County, for these adjoining tracts. In most instances the large property boundaries were fairly easy to recover and plot. The deeds once found, we transcribed the relevant parts of the old handwritten descriptions — often a tedious process, especially if the handwriting of the original clerk-copyist was too florid — and converted the distances into feet and tenths of feet. At the period of our interest (ca. 1790–1825) the lengths of lines on the land were usually given in the old surveyors' units of chains, links, and poles. Although not commonly used today, these units are the basis for the modern unit of land area in the United States, the acre, which measures 43,560 square feet or 10 square chains (a chain was 66 feet long, divided into 100 links each 7.92 inches long; a pole was one-fourth of a chain, or 16.5 feet—that is, 5.5 yards, sometimes also called one rod). After transcribing the handwritten descriptions and converting the distances, it was relatively quick and easy to punch the information into the computer, and to compare the geometry of any one tract with that of adjoining tracts.

Sometimes, as in the case of the large tract owned by Bryant Kittrell to the southwest of the village (where some of Mitchell's favorite botanical localities were found), the difficulty was not how to plot the boundaries of the property itself, but how to determine where it lay in relation to other tracts. Since the common boundary between the Kittrell lands and the University lands had no shared corner, it was impossible to tell directly how the two parcels were connected. Other information had to be sought. Fortunately, the old deeds not only provide information on the bearings, dimensions, and ownership of adjoining tracts, but often include information about natural landmarks used to identify the property boundaries by inspection on the ground. Kittrell's deed noted where the boundaries of his land touched on or ran with Morgan's Creek or the branches that feed into it. By plotting the deed and overlaying it on the topographic map, it was possible to move the plot on its north-south and east-west axes and find a location where the respective points "on the South side of the Creek" and "the South side of the branch" coincided with the existing topography.

In this way our map gradually took shape. For the most part the old tracts were carefully described and could be reconstructed, but some descriptions were too vague or confusing to plot, like that of the Craig land to the west of the village. These had to be plotted by inference. Thus, as we entered the tracts surrounding the Craig property into the computer, the boundaries of the tract itself became evident. After the basic information on property boundary lines was obtained and plotted, the next step was to plot the natural features of creeks and branches onto the map. These were traced directly from the USGS topographic sheet. In areas now covered by the waters of University Lake and Eastwood Lake, the approximate courses of the stream beds were reconstructed from the surrounding topography.

More difficult to reconstruct were the roads into and around the village of Chapel Hill in Mitchell's time. Sometimes information on the location of these roads was provided in deed descriptions, but not in sufficient quantities to permit us to show long continuous portions of the older roads on our map. To improve our understanding of their whereabouts we made use of the information provided by early maps of Chapel Hill and its suroundings, in particular the "Daniel" map of 1792 (reproduced in Henderson, 1949, facing p. 22). An approximate scale was derived by using the deed distances for the boundaries of the University donations and comparing them with the same boundaries as plotted on the Daniel map. The roads were then scaled onto the transparent worksheets for our new map. A second important source used to verify road locations was the first (1946) USGS map of the Chapel Hill Quadrangle; we have concluded that road locations in post–World War II Chapel Hill had changed remarkably little since Mitchell's day.[1] Even today the approaches to Chapel Hill correspond closely to the roads shown on the earliest maps (see the entry "Chapel Hill" in Appendix C, below).

The layout and dimensions of the streets and lots of Mitchell's Chapel Hill were plotted from information found on two carefully drawn early maps. The older of the two, now in the University Archives, is entitled "Plan of the Village of Chapel Hill" and is dated September 4, 1817 — that is, it was prepared just before Mitchell's arrival at the University. It numbers the lots in accordance with the numbers assigned before their sale in 1793, identifies some of the owners, and shows the location of the University's few buildings, including the Preparatory School. It also specifies the dimensions of the village lots and streets, and these (which correspond quite closely to the street and block dimensions of modern Chapel Hill) were used to plot the lots onto our map.

The other map of which we made much use, preserved in the North Carolina Collection at the University, is dated 1852 and is annotated in a hand very similar to that of Elisha Mitchell; we suspect, indeed, that it was he who prepared it. This map reveals the continuing subdivision of the original lots, and it also supplies the names of streets in use at that time. Although the individual lots are not numbered, nor their dimensions supplied, the widths, lengths, and bearings of the streets are given, as well as information on the corporate limits "according to the Charter" of the town. Intersections of the village streets with roads entering the town are also shown with some precision, and these helped to confirm our inferences about such roads, as drawn from the Daniel map of 1792. Both the map of 1817 and that of 1852 provided new information about the names and locations of streams and springs in the area, and the Daniel map indicated the approximate locations of McCauley's mill, Yeargain's mill, and Jones's [= Craig's] mill, all of which figure in early deeds and are included on our Map 1.

The information taken from early maps and deeds thus allowed us to create a hand-drawn map at the USGS scale of 1: 24000, a map incorporating notes on the various corner descriptions, ownership of lots, and other details. We next transferred this hand-drawn map into a computer with CAD (Computer Assisted Drafting) capability, which allowed for the editing and revising necessary to produce our final version.

Here it must be emphasized that although we attempted to keep our map as mathematically accurate as possible, some elements of imprecision were inevitably introduced. The large acreage involved made it prohibitive for us, in terms of

---

[1]The copy of the 1946 map in the Ayers surveying files had been annotated in the course of surveys done for the University in the 1950s and 1960s, and the UNC boundaries of that period that were marked on it have helped confirm our plots of certain boundaries of the original tracts.

time and expense, to carry out new field surveys with modern techniques. For small tracts, by scaling the beginning points of our map from tax maps plotted at 1 inch = 100 feet, we could allow for a margin of error of plus or minus 5 feet in 100. Since the contiguous original grants to the trustees included approximately 835 acres, we had to scale from the most detailed available USGS maps, drawn at a scale of 1 inch = 2000 feet, with the result that the accuracy with which any specific point can be located is approximately 50 feet, plus or minus.

In addition to the errors in individual deed descriptions, and the probable error in scaling accuracy, further confusion is created by a deed overlap of approximately 400 feet between the two tracts acquired independently by the university from Hardy Morgan (tracts 15 and 16). This overlap became apparent when we transferred the village streets and lots from the 1817 "Plan of the Village" to our map, and compared them with present-day streets as shown in the USGS map. Using our established baseline along the Hardy Morgan property (tract 17) as a match-line, we found that the street systems on the respective maps were offset by the same east-west distance as the deed overlap. Apparently both the author of the 1817 plan and the author of the 1852 map were unaware of the discrepancy, although the overlap is clearly shown on another map of the university and village, this one unsigned and undated, which is on file in the University Archives.

Finally, any deed that described a parcel other than a square or a rectangle was almost sure to include some mathematical error, because of the limitations of the available surveying instruments of the time (usually a compass, a chain, and possibly a sextant). Because of the difficulties of running long straight lines through the woods with compass and chain, and because of the lack of correction for slope in the measurement of distances across hills and valleys, the larger tracts often have greater errors in their descriptions than do the smaller ones. Modern computer software can calculate the amount of error in an old description, but the only method of determining just where the errors lie, short of actually surveying the property, is to make an educated guess by comparing the overlays of deed plots with existing modern maps. By comparing corner designations of points on creeks, branches, and roadways to modern topographic maps, we have been able to make some assumptions about the accuracy of various deeds, and to adjust our map accordingly.

The benefits of having the map on a computer disk were most apparent during the final editing. Changes could be made without erasing and then redrawing a hard copy. Trial revisions could be plotted and compared to the topographic map before becoming permanently incorporated into our map. CAD also allows for the layering of data, so that certain kinds of information can be displayed or repressed on the video terminal or plotter for ease in editing and drafting. Storage on floppy disks also facilitated the publication of the final map, since the publisher could work directly with the disk's electronic data, thus eliminating errors in scale or relative size.

We hope that our Map 1 will be useful not only in conjunction with this study of Mitchell's Chapel Hill, but also as a basis of reference for future studies of the village as it once was. Given the recent advances in surveying technology, many of the approximate boundaries shown on our map could be identified with much more accuracy if two or more old corners or other distinctive field information were to be located. Global Positioning Systems (GPS) using data from satellites now allow the surveyor to set up instruments on the ground that can generate exact grid coordinates, corrected for the curvature of the earth and on a true-north system, enabling the user to determine not only the precise position of any individual point, but the relationships between points located at great distances from one another. At a more mundane but still quite accurate level, many old corners could be tied to the extensive sanitary sewer system in Chapel Hill, since North Carolina coordinates are on file for each manhole located within the jurisdiction of the Orange Water and Sewer Authority. Finally, much additional information remains to be unearthed from the descriptions on file with the Register of Deeds in Hillsborough, by tracing the chain of title for modern lots or other tracts and using the tax maps and the USGS topographic maps, as we have in the present study, to reconstruct a part of the past. We look forward hopefully to future studies of old Chapel Hill.

APPENDIX C
AN ECLECTIC INDEX TO MITCHELL'S PLACES AND PEOPLE

Barbee. Christopher Barbee (1738/40–1834). One of the original donors to the University (see Appendix D, tract 14[1]), who lived east of the village, on what Battle (1907, p. 194; 1912, p. 770) called "The Mountain," "a prominent landmark" visible from the hill on which Gimghoul Castle now stands, and about 4 km (2 1/2) miles east of it. The hill in question is in Durham County, east of where Bolin Creek and Booker Creek converge to become Little Creek, the latter continuing into Jordan Lake, passing about 500 m north of "The Mountain." Presumably when Mitchell wrote "down toward Barbees on Bollings Creek" he was going in this direction, as when he noted "down Bolling's Creek to Old Mr. Barbees." Doubtless "Old Mr. Barbee" was Mitchell's way of distinguishing him from his son William Barbee, one-time Steward and later also Superintendent of the University.

Barbee's (or "**Barby's**") **mill** (later Cave's, King's, or Oldham's mill, according to Battle, 1912, p. 766) and its surroundings on Morgan Creek were among Mitchell's favorite botanizing grounds. Mitchell referred once to "Barbees eastern mill" with the implication that Barbee had another mill on Bolin Creek, but we have not been able to confirm this.

Bevil. This is Elisha Bevill; see **Lee**, below, as well as the text above, pp. 57, 68. Bevill's land was near the northwestern border of tract 9 on our Map 1, "on the waters of Presswood creek" near what is now Eastwood Lake.

Bollings (or **Bowlings**) **Creek**. This is the modern Bolin Creek, named after Benjamin Bolin, an early land-holder. The name has been corrupted variously, in the older land-deeds and more recently in names for streets and suburban developments, to Bones Creek (1788), Bolings Creek (1788), Bens or Ben's Creek (1788, 1807), Bowlings Creek (1809), Boland's or Ben Bolen's Creek (1815), Bowlin's Creek (1821), Bolling's Creek (1826), and Borland's Creek (1798, 1843). In

---
[1] In the text that follows all references to numbered tracts are to those described in Appendix D and shown on Map 1, which see inside the back cover of this work. The references to localities or people that we quote from Mitchell's ledger (EM2) can be identified through the index at the end of this work.

modern times it is officially back to Bolin Creek, but today's "Bowling Creek Road" still testifies to the earlier confusion. Mitchell botanized along the creek on numerous occasions.

Caldwell. Joseph Caldwell (1773–1835). President of the University. In 1818 President Caldwell lived in the house at the southeast corner of Raleigh Street and Franklin Street (Battle, 1907, p. 271), one of the two houses to the east of Raleigh Street on that side. Mitchell's references in 1820 and 1821 to "Mrs. Caldwells garden" and "Dr. Caldwells yard" are presumably self-explanatory. The house originally meant for President Caldwell was on lot 2 on the original plan of the village, at the northeast corner of Columbia Street and Cameron Avenue (then called College Street, or merely "the Avenue"). The location of the house is shown on a plan of the village, drawn by an unknown artist between 1797 and 1812 (Henderson, 1949, facing p. 56). Mitchell himself lived in the original "President's house" from soon after his arrival in Chapel Hill until the end of his life.

In 1805 Caldwell bought a tract of land west of the college (tract 20), not far from his original lot in the village, and when Mitchell wrote that he passed through "Dr. Caldwells field toward Kittrells" he may well have been crossing that tract. Another reference to this property speaks of traveling "through the Presidents field and down the branch." The branch presumably would have been the one behind present Lincoln School, near the line between Chapel Hill and Carrboro.

Cave. Dr. Belfield William Cave (1796–?). The Dr. Cave who identified Mitchell's plant (EM2, p. 122) was married to William Barbee's daughter Delia. His son, also Belfield William Cave, graduated from the University in 1848 (Battle 1907, pp. 30, 310).

Chapel Hill. The location of the original site of the village, the original subdivision and sale of lots, and the orientation of the streets are all discussed in the present text, chiefly in Appendixes A and E. Much information on these matters, in addition to that taken from the old property deeds, was obtained from early maps of Chapel Hill. This last was especially true as regards the locations of the old roads into the village, which are only incidentally and sketchily mentioned in the property deeds. We found that the Daniel map of 1792 was particularly useful in this respect; another valuable source was an early (1946) version of the Chapel Hill sheet of the USGS topographic map. We assumed that the locations of the roads in Mitchell's time, and in Chapel Hill in the years immediately following World War II, were much the same, considering the relatively small growth of the town during that long period, and the economic hardships imposed by the Civil War, by Reconstruction, by the Great Depression, and by World War II itself.

It transpired that many present-day roads approaching the town do indeed seem to correspond to the roads shown in the Daniel map. West of town, the road designated as the "road to McCauley's Mill" is near the location of present-day Jones Ferry Road, and the "road to Salisberry" seems to run generally west from near the site of the present Carolina Inn, to modern Main Street, Weaver Street, and old Hillsborough Street, in Carrboro. An unnamed road intersecting the others and shown passing "Piper's House" corresponds to present-day Old Fayetteville Road. To the south of town, the "Road from Chatham Courthouse [Pittsboro] to Petersburg" probably follows the former course of Smith Level Road. The latter, shown on the 1946 USGS map as crooked and winding, was the road to the plantation of U.S. Congressman Dr. James Smith, who built his home there in the 1840s (the house is still standing just west of the road). The northern portion of the same road, as shown on the Daniel map, corresponds to present-day Old Pittsboro Road, just west of Greensboro Street in Carrboro. To the east of Chapel Hill, the road shown as "road to seat [of] Government — Wake" would have followed the modern Gimghoul Road as far as the point where the rocky descent made a direct road impossible.

The principal road from Chapel Hill to the northeast is shown on the Daniel map as crossing the "Salisberry road" somewhat southwest of the center of Barbee's donation (tract 14) — that is to say, near the site of the present Carolina Inn on the University campus. Here at the crossing was the presumed location of the old "Chapel of Ease" for which the hill was named. From the crossing the road continued northeastward across the campus, passing behind (south of) the Morehead Planetarium, through the northwestern part of the Arboretum and through old town lots 19 (the current presidential residence) and 21 (today the Kyser house), crossing Franklin Street near the corner with Boundary Street and finally to near the intersection of Rosemary and Glenburnie. At that point the hill drops off steeply into the valley of Bolin Creek, and even by 1792 the map shows the road avoiding this by making an abrupt curve to the right, evidently about where Franklin Street curves the same way today. This old trade route to Petersburg seems to have fallen into disuse as soon as (or even before) the village streets were established, but portions of it are shown on old deeds, usually under the name of the "great road," passing from the campus down the hill to Bolin Creek somewhat to the east of modern Franklin Street, and then more or less along present Old Oxford Road to beyond the boundaries of modern Chapel Hill. For references to the Great Road see Appendix D, tracts 7, 8, 9, 13, 15, 16, 21.

Craig. Mitchell refers several times to the "Craig" property as lying west of the village on the way to Morgan Creek. The Orange County deeds mention both "James" and "John" Craig as owners of lands west of the village, which abutted the five-acre tract (tract 13) given to the University in 1792 by James Craig, Sr. (d. 1827). Most of the perimeter of these Craig lands can be securely established (tract 12), though we have not been able to fix their northwestern boundary, and Mitchell must have been speaking of some part of them. His note, "To Major Hendersons fields. Saw a good many plants coming into flower — in particular a certain succulent one in Craigs field," suggests that it was necessary to pass through Craig's field (cf. tract 12) to reach Henderson's fields (tract 19), and this is confirmed by a later note, saying "Major Hendersons field beyond Craigs."

According to Battle (1907, p. 32), James Craig's home was "in the extreme western part of the village" and was "for many years a favorite boarding house for those not adverse to long walks." Perhaps this domestic association explains why Mitchell once refers specifically to "Mrs. Craig's house" and another time to "Mrs. Craig's fields."

Daniel. John Daniel. A long-time resident of Chapel Hill, active during Mitchell's botanical years. One of the original donors to the University (see tract 23), Daniel also made the first known survey and map of Chapel Hill, dated 1792. According to Battle (1907, p. 30) John Daniel lived "on the road between the mill and the village." Mitchell referred to the Barbee-Daniel house, the hillside south of the house, the spring below it, and "the field below the house near the branch."

Henderson. Pleasant Henderson (1756–1840). West of President Caldwell's land and north of Bryant Kittrell's, Henderson's land (tract 19) is occasionally mentioned by Mitchell: e.g., "on Major Hendersons plantation near the house" and "rambled out to the steep rocks south of Major Hendersons plantation." Major Henderson (the title came from his service in the American Revolution) for a time after 1815 also owned land north of Bolin Creek (tract 2). He lived in the village for some years.

Hillsborough. The county seat of Orange County, 12 miles north of Chapel Hill and in 1820 already a well-established town. There were at least two traveled roads between Chapel Hill and Hillsborough. One (the "near road to Hillsborough"), a continuation of what was even in Mitchell's time called Hillsborough Street, crossed the deep valley of Bolin Creek and continued northward somewhat to the west of the modern road, eventually joining an old established road that came in from the south. The other route from Chapel Hill followed the old Petersburg road to the northeast for a time before turning toward Hillsborough from the southeast, via New Hope. Mitchell may well have gone to Hillsborough on numerous occasions, but on only two of these did he leave notes about plants. The first of these excursions seems to have been in the period June 17–27, 1820, and the second in September of the same year. (We have assumed that both were in 1820 because of their position in the pages of the ledger and because the dates fit neatly into periods when Mitchell was not recording any excursions in the vicinity of Chapel Hill; it remains entirely possible that one or both trips took place in some other year.)

From near or on the way to Hillsborough, Mitchell mentions plants from "Mr. Yarboroughs meadow"; he found "Wisteria speciosa of Nutall" on "Dr. Webbs arbour," saying "I know not whence it came." He mentions "the Devils Turnip Patch on the road to Hillsborough." Plants from the "road to New Hope" and "beyond New Hope and near Hillsborough" perhaps came from one of the two above trips. We have not attempted to identify these people and places any further, although "Dr. Webb" may well be the same person who bought a portion of Chapel Hill town lot 10 in 1821 (see Appendix E).

Following a mention of Mr. Yarborough's meadow dated June 27, [?1820], there is an inserted note, "July 7, 1837 in the ascent of the Hill to Mr. Pott's." The note may be quite extraneous, but we see no way to be sure. The land that Jacob Potts bought from the University in 1826 (tract 1) lay athwart present Airport Road, and Mitchell may well have been referring to the very considerable ascent from Bolin Creek to the top of the hill there.

Hooper. Mitchell referred in 1820 to a plant "in flower in Mrs. Hoopers garden" (EM2, p. 115). William Hooper (1792–1876) was Mitchell's colleague, Professor of Ancient Languages, and from about 1817 to 1822 lived on the south side of Franklin Street, next door to President Caldwell (Battle 1907, page 271). He owned the property after 1819 (see under Lot 21 in Appendix E), but as shown in our Map 2, his name had become associated with it as early as 1817.

Jones, Col. In Mitchell's copy of Pursh's *Flora*, p. 107, under *Ptelea trifoliata*, is his pencilled note "Col. Jones' Plantation", with date June 17, 1821. In a second note, this time in his ledger under date April 23, 1822, Mitchell mentions having seen a plant on April 1st, "beside Haw River near the ferry to Col. Jones'". It is tempting to make the connection between this second note and modern Jones Ferry Road, which begins in downtown Carrboro and now crosses the Haw River on a bridge. A bridge known as "Jones' Bridge" already existed on the site in 1865, but we find no earlier mention of a ferry there. It is also tempting to assume that the "Col. Jones" of Jones' Ferry was Edmond Jones, who had fought in the Revolutionary War, and was one of the original donors to the University, but we have not been able to verify this. Edmond Jones the donor bought and sold much land in southern Orange County between 1792 and 1802, though at least in 1802 he was referred to in a deed as a resident of the "County of Chatham", and Battle (1907, p. 33) says that this Edmond Jones "established himself [in Chatham County] on Ephraim's Creek...midway between Siler City and Ore Hill", which would appear to have been 20 miles south of the Haw River. Perhaps a search of Chatham County land-deeds (which we have not made) would better establish the site of his plantation, and even his ferry.

Kittrell. This name, and that of Merritt, are the ones that occur the most frequently among Mitchell's notes. Bryant Kittrell (?1774–1837) owned more than 500 acres (tract 28) on both sides of Morgan Creek, above William Merritt's holdings. Mitchell refers regularly to a number of features of this tract, especially the fish traps set in the creek and the ford that provided Mitchell with his usual crossing place over it. See also **Maples**, below.

Laurel Hill. Several Laurel Hills (now often called "Rhododendron bluffs") still exist on the steep south side of the valley of Morgan Creek. Mitchell referred several times to his visits to Laurel Hill, e.g., "Laurel Hill on the rock with Mitchella repens," once at least to "Laurel Hill above Kittrells on the creek," and once to what was evidently another such locality, "from Merits down the creek on the other side," where he found the *Rhododendron* at the Whetstone Rocks. Battle (1912, p. 766) refers to one Laurel Hill near Barbee's mill. At present this last locality supports the largest known population of *Rhododendron* along the creek.

Lee. This was evidently James B. Leigh, who lived on the headwaters of Schoolhouse Branch, west of Elisha Bevill who bought adjoining land on Presswood (now Booker) Creek from John Craig, 3 Dec. 1816 (DB 18/202); see text above, pp. 57, 68. The holdings of both Leigh and Bevill adjoined the western and northwestern borders of tract 9, in what is now the residential area around Eastwood Lake.

Lewis. This probably was Orrin Lewis, who lived in the village, toward the eastern end, and apparently owned land on the hill between there and Bolin Creek. Mitchell referred to "N.E. from the hill near the creek on the south side. West of Mr. Lewis's"; and "Mr. Lewis's creek."

McCauley. Mathew McCauley (1750–1832) and his older brother William (d. ca. 1826) were among the original donors of land to the University (tracts 35 and 1, respectively). The McCauley home and McCauley's mill were in the valley of Morgan Creek not far from the dam that now impounds University Lake. The "road to McCauley's mill" as shown on old maps was near the present location of Jones Ferry Road, the continuation of Main Street in Carrboro. From Mitchell's notes: "Mr. Kittrell's field up towards McCauleys"; "back of Kittrells. Crossed the creek at the usual place. Went to McCauleys and came in the road home."

Maples, the. This was Mitchell's name for a locality on Morgan Creek where it passed through Bryant Kittrell's property, a locality to which he returned several times and where he found several plants that interested him. On April 21, 1821, "from Merits Meadow up to the Maples at the turn of Creek" he found *Orontium aquaticum, Pedicularis canadensis, Arisaema triphyllum*, and, what intrigued him the most, a plant that he took to be *Ellisia nyctelea*; he wrote, "Ellisia is at the corner of the fence near the Maples." In a note the next year, April 17, 1822, on a visit to "the bend in Morgan's Creek at the Maples," he said, "Ellisia nyctelea grows plentifully by the side of a rock in the field about a half mile above this and is in flower." As noted above, his plant was probably not *Ellisia*, but may well have been hydrophyllaceous.

Merritt. William Henry Merritt (17xx – ca. 1829) owned about 500 acres (tracts 29–31) on both sides of Morgan Creek, including a mill seat (tract 31) that he had purchased from John Morgan in 1787. The mill, which stood on the north side of the creek just below the Pittsboro road, was according to Battle (1912, p. 767) "a famous flour mill before the railroads came." It was known in the early part of the twentieth century as Purefoy's Mill. Apparently no vestige of it now remains, it having been washed away by a great flood in August, 1924.

Mitchell. Elisha Mitchell (1793–1857). There are occasional references to plants seen "close by the corner of our yard" or "in my garden." Mitchell lived in the original "President's house," on the northeast corner of Columbia Street and Cameron Avenue (see **Caldwell**, above), in the house described by Battle (1907, p. 252) as "nearest the University buildings on the west." Until 1822–1823, when Old West was built (Henderson, 1949, pp. 84–85) there were no University buildings between the house and Old East, which seemed far enough that Mitchell would note the discovery of a plant "between my house and college." A drawing showing the house is reproduced by Henderson (1949, facing p. 64; our fig. 1, p. 4). Probably in 1835, Mitchell noted a species of *Liatris* "in my field in the moist untilled new ground." He had begun to buy land near the village, mostly in the valley of Bolin Creek, at least as early as 1821 (tract 3), and this particular field is otherwise unidentified.

Norwood. Mitchell found what he took to be *Crataegus pyrifolia* "near Mr. Norwood's on New Hope [Creek]." We know nothing further about Mr. Norwood. The roads to Hillsborough crossed New Hope Creek on the way from Chapel Hill.

Olmsted. Denison Olmsted (1791–1859). There is one reference in Mitchell's notes (April, 1825) to a plant "by the side of Mr. Olmsteds house." Olmsted, Mitchell's fellow professor until 1825, bought in June 1820 the house still known as the "Widow Puckett house," on the north side of Franklin Street across from Professor Hooper's house; see below, Appendix E, Lot 22.

Preparatory School. Mitchell several times mentions botanizing in the vicinity. See the text above, p. 67, and **Taylor**, below. Henderson (1949, pp. 40–44) tells the story of this short-lived department of the University, which began operation in 1796 and was discontinued in 1819. The building, which stood in the similarly short-lived Grand Avenue, was completed in 1802. Henderson locates it in modern terms as near the southeast corner of the intersection of Henderson and Rosemary streets, between that corner and the Presbyterian church.

Scott's Hole. In Mitchell's time this seems to have been a permanent body of water, evidently with a fringe of willows and other shrubs around it, and some aquatics in and around it. Mitchell visited it first on March 10, 1820, when he referred to it as "the pond S.E. from College" and found "in the pond" what he took to be the *Laurus diospyrus* of Pursh and Nuttall. On Feb. 22, 1822, he returned to what must have been the same pond: "Down about Scotts Hole — ascertained the shrub in the pond to be Laurus geniculata of Pursh and Elliott"; as discussed above (pp. 11, 25–26), his identification seems to have been the correct one, and this was an extraordinary find. He returned to this site — "down the Raleigh road and over to Scott's Hole"— several times in later years, once referring to "Solomon Morgan's field near Scotts Hole"; this is not a very precise locality, as Solomon Morgan owned much of the land along Morgan Creek southeast of the village. Later references to Scott's Hole, made by other people, place it near the junction of Morgan Creek and Meeting of the Waters Creek (cf. Henderson, 1949, p. 23, note 4) and probably within walking distance of Solomon Morgan's home. The name Scott's Hole appears on herbarium labels as late as 1916 or 1920, and older residents of Chapel Hill remember swimming in Scott's Hole. The consensus seems to be that such a pond could have been formed originally by the cutting off of a meander in Morgan Creek. The pond itself, however, seems to have disappeared, perhaps covered by earth-moving operations during the construction of the University golf course and the sewage-treatment plant.

Taylor. See **Bollings Creek**. Mitchell found much of interest to the north of the village, between the Preparatory School and the creek, on "Mr. Taylors" property: "NW on Maj. Hendersons and below Prep. School on Mr. Taylors land"; "Mr Taylors field below the Prep. Schoolhouse"; "in the same field in the lately cleared side hill"; "side of small streams north of the village"; "Taylors meadow east from hill in the old field"; "Bollings Creek in Mr. Taylors field"; "Mr. Taylors field Bollings Creek"; "in the swamp in the field of Mr. Taylor field beyond Bollings Creek." It is not always clear whether the Taylor in question was John Taylor, Sr. (1747–1826), or his son Thomas H. Taylor (?1786–?1841), as both of them owned land in the vicinity about this time.

The land on the "side hill" below the "Prep. Schoolhouse" was presumably below the north end of modern Henderson Street in the direction of Bolin Creek, still a springy area, still incompletely developed, apparently first cleared in 1819 or 1820.

Watson. A reference to a plant found "near Watson's shop" follows immediately after some paragraphs devoted to Mitchell's trip to Hillsborough in September 1820, but we have not identified Mr. Watson, unless he may have been the William Watson who lived somewhere on 4-acre lot III, north of Rosemary Street, near the business district of Chapel Hill, before 1839.

Webb, Dr. See **Hillsborough**.

Whetstone Rocks. Evidently an outcrop (or perhaps more than one such outcrop) on the steep south side of Morgan Creek, presumably on one of the so-called Laurel Hills, where *Rhododendron catawbiense* grows naturally. Mitchell once mentioned finding the *Rhododendron* at Whetstone Rocks, "from Merits down the creek on the other side." On one day he "walked with the ladies to the Whetstone Rocks," this suggesting that it was not a long or difficult walk to the rocks, from the road leading up to the University. See **Laurel Hill**.

Whyte. Probably in 1835, Mitchell noted that he found *Prenanthes alba* "in Mr. Whytes field." We have not identified Mr. Whyte further, unless he was the Thomas E. Whyte who sold village lot 18 in 1850.

Yarborough. See **Hillsborough**.

APPENDIX D
THE NUMBERED TRACTS SHOWN ON MAP 1[1]

Tracts are in the town of Chapel Hill unless otherwise noted, and have been numbered arbitrarily, more or less from west to east and north to south. References to these tracts, as described in the Deed Books in the office of the Orange County Register of Deeds, Hillsborough, are cited below by book and page (e.g., "DB 11/287" for Deed Book 11, page 287).

The central part of our map indicates particularly the area occupied by the parcels of land that were donated to the trustees of the University. The background for this has been discussed at length by Battle (1907, pp. 3–33). The charter of the University was granted by the General Assembly of North Carolina in December 1789, a month after North Carolina became a state. The same act established a Board of Trustees as the principal governing body. The trustees at once undertook a search for the most appropriate (and most feasible) site for the University. A group of Commissioners, appointed by the trustees in August 1792, soon narrowed down the choice of sites to five counties in the central part of the state (Wake, Granville, Johnston, Chatham, Orange). The Commissioners met in Pittsboro, Chatham County, early in November, and compared sites in Chatham and Orange County. The report on this meeting (November 6) referred to offers from various citizens, totaling 1290 acres of land, of which 840 were on the Chapel Hill or nearby. Reports for November 7–9 listed twelve men who collectively agreed to donate more than 1200 acres to the trustees, on condition that the University be established on the Chapel Hill. All of the donors eventually made good on their promises, altogether conveying almost 1400 acres on behalf of the new University. Eight tracts, comprising some 835 acres, formed a contiguous area on the Chapel Hill itself (our numbered tracts 13–17 and 21–23), and the others were nearby in Orange County. Although a few of the deeds to the land were dated at the time of the meeting in Pittsboro, early in November 1792, most of them were proved in court in 1796. All the contiguous tracts are shown on our map, and are described briefly below by number, as is also William McCauley's donation (tract 1). Three donations — those of Thomas Connally, John Hogan, and Mathew McCauley — are numbered (tracts 33–35), and are briefly described below, but are not mapped.

Tract 1. William McCauley to the trustees, 6 October 1796, 100 acres "on the waters of Boling's creek," for a consideration of 5 shillings (DB 5/618). This land

---
[1] See map and caption inside back cover.

was at the time relatively remote from the proposed site of the University, and separated from it by the deep valley of Bolin Creek. The University sold it to Jacob Potts, 14 August 1826 (DB 23/33). It adjoins tract 4 to the north. It lies mostly east of present Airport Road, with the northwest corner near Horace Williams Airport. Part of it having reverted to University ownership, it includes the property at the Physical Plant west of Airport Road.

Tract 2. Jessey [sic] Riggsby and Alexander Strain to Samuel Love, 31 January 1801, 132 acres on "Boland's" Creek (DB 11/287). Sold by Robert Love to Pleasant Henderson, 2 November 1815, this time on "Boland" Creek (DB 16/115). Essentially the same tract, re-surveyed and augmented, was sold by James Webb to Elisha Mitchell, 25 May 1843, on "Borland's" Creek (DB 30/224). The tract was bounded on the south by Craig's lands (tract 12) and on the east by tract 4, which after 1810 belonged to Joseph Caldwell. Bolin Creek crossed the lower third of tract 2 more or less from WNW to ESE (past the confluence with Tanbark Branch) and thence crossed easterly through nearly the middle of tract 4. The northwest corner of tract 2 is approximately at present Estes Drive, ca 1.3 km west of Airport Road.

Tract 3. Thomas H. Taylor to Elisha Mitchell, 8 November 1821, 41 acres (DB 19/215). This is a portion of the original tract 4 acquired by Joseph Caldwell in 1810, comprising the land south of Bolin Creek at the west end of tract 4, west of present Airport Road near the north end of Columbia Street extended.

Tract 4. Benjamin Yeargan[2] to Joseph Caldwell, 9 August 1810, 523 1/2 acres "on the north side of the village of the University" (DB 13/389). This is evidently much the same tract, modified and augmented, as the rectangular tract sold by Mark Patterson to Benjamin Yeargains [sic], 25 February 1788, an estimated 450 acres on "Bens Creek, beginning from Benj. Bowlins corner" (DB 4/37). Most of the steepest valley of the creek lies within this tract, which is one of the largest and most irregularly shaped on our map. Because of the steep slopes both north and south of Bolin Creek, much of the area is still wooded, with increasing residential development, from near the mouth of Tanyard Branch, east to the foot of Elizabeth Street where that descends nearly to creek-level; the southeast extension of the tract includes present Tenney Circle, and Franklin Street nearly halfway down the hill.

Tract 5. Benjamin Yeargan to Whitted & Craig, 4 December 1805, 6 acres "adjoining the land of Benjamin Yeargan and the trustees" (DB 12/342). The adjoining lands mentioned are tract 4 (which still belonged to Yeargan in 1805), and tracts 14 and 15, University property. Tract 5 was a narrow strip only 200 feet wide, on a fairly steep slope, seemingly of little use as an agricultural area or a homesite, between present Tenney Circle and the apartments on the declivity of Airport Road north of Chapel Hill. The buyers are identified only as "Whitted & Craig", but when they sold the same lot to James Putney on 25 July 1810 (DB 14/27), their names were signed as William Whitted and John [Jn.] Craig. As a part of the same transaction, they sold a part of Village lot no. 10, which see.

---

[2]The name is variously spelled. In this index it is spelled as it appears on the deeds. Personally he seems to have favored the spelling Yeargain.

Tract 6. Benjamin Yeargan to John Craig, 2 November 1807, 81.5 acres on "Ben's creek" (DB 13/108). This adjoins tract 4 on its southern and southwestern boundaries, and tract 9 on the northeast. It occupied much of the area to the southeast from present Estes Park school, south of Estes Drive and north of Bolin Creek. The boundary between tracts 6 and 9 was Schoolhouse Branch, now essentially dry, then running southeasterly, north of present Estes Drive, to its junction with Bolin Creek just west of the Franklin Street bridge. Southeast of tract 6 is the site of Craig's mill tract (tract 7).

Tract 7. Hardy Morgan to Edmond Jones, 29 March 1792, 10 acres, "together with a Saw Mill on the farm by Hardy Morgan's and by him built" (DB 5/20). The Daniel map of 1792 shows the Jones sawmill on the south side of Bollings Creek, west of the Petersburg road. Edmond Jones sold the same tract to James Patterson, 18 November 1793 (DB 5/122). Patterson sold the same to George Johnston and Samuel Hopkins, 25 January 1797, "including a sawmill formerly the property of Hardy Morgan" (DB 6/320). The deed indicates that the northeast corner is on "Bowland's Creek," the east side bounded by the "old road" (i.e., the "great road," to Petersburg), and the west side following Yeargan's line (tract 6), crossing the creek at some undesignated point. We have not found a record of when Craig acquired the mill site. As early as 1807 it was referred to as "John Craig's Mill tract" (DB 6/320). We have assumed that the ten acres were in the form of a square, more or less, but the deeds fail to state the dimensions.

Tract 8. Lemuel Morgan to John Craig, 27 December 1809, 15 acres "on Bowlings Creek adjoining said Craig's Mill seat, beginning on the [south] bank of the creek below the great road and mill" (DB 14/510). This narrow tract on a north–south axis adjoins the east edge of tract 4, and its north end adjoins Craig's mill tract (tract 7). It is interesting that the east side of tract 8 runs with the "great road" for the southern two-thirds of its length, and after a jog to the east continues parallel to the road as far north as Bolin Creek, crossing the creek almost at the present Franklin Street bridge. The southern part of the tract was located on the slope ascending from the creek to the village, between present Roosevelt Drive and Franklin Street.

Tract 9. John Morgan to John Craig, 16 November 1811, 513 acres on "Wilkes or Presswood creek" (DB 14/512). This large tract lies south and southeast of present Eastwood Lake. It was bordered on the southwest by the course of Schoolhouse Branch, and by tract 6, and extends east and northeast approximately to the junction of present routes 15-501 and Erwin Road. Presswood (now Booker) Creek ran almost north-south through the property. To the northeast of where the property line crossed the creek, it followed what is now Old Oxford Road, which is evidently a remnant of the "great road" to Petersburg. The creek is now much diminished, and passes unnoticed under the Eastgate Mall, in the southeastern part of tract 9. All or most of the shopping centers associated with Eastgate and with Elliot Road would lie within these boundaries.

Tract 10. Samuel Hopkins to William Nunn, 12 July 1799, 83 acres (DB 8/193). In Carrboro, a rectangle bounded on the east by Greensboro Street, north almost to where that street turns northwest at Pleasant Avenue, then west beyond the junction of Hillsboro Road and route 54, then south 103 poles (ca. 1700 feet or

1/3 mile), then east again. The southeast corner of the rectangular tract was not a part of the property, but was filled by Alexander Piper's donation, tract 11. The old mill village in Carrboro, in the northwest quadrant of the Weaver Street and North Greensboro areas, covered parts of tracts 10 and 11, and the present Carrboro Town Hall is about at the southwest corner of tract 10.

Tract 11. Alexander Piper's donation to the Trustees, 18 October 1796, 20 acres, for a consideration of 5 shillings (DB 5/614). Sold by the Trustees to John Craig for $40.00, 30 September 1837 (DB 28/272). In Carrboro, not contiguous with the principal area on which the University and the village of Chapel Hill were founded. A rectangle, comprising a corner cut out of tract 10, bounded on the east (40 poles, or ca. 1/8 mile) by Greensboro Street, with its southeast corner on the road to McCauley's mill. The Daniel map shows the road forking at that corner, and that fork is evidently very near the fork of present Main Street and Weaver Street, not far from the railroad in eastern Carrboro.

Tract 12. Holdings of John Craig and James Craig. We have not located the early deeds for these holdings, but their boundary can be almost completely reconstructed from the properties that surrounded them. The tract occupied much of the land from just west of the center of Chapel Hill to Greensboro Street in Carrboro, north almost to Bolin Creek, and south almost to the present western extension of McCauley Street. A projection of modern Airport Road south to Cameron Avenue would approximate the eastern boundary. The southern edge of the Craig land (in 1798) was a common boundary with tracts 20 and 21, and the western boundary was Greensboro Street, where it ran south at least from the northeast corner of Alexander Piper's donation (tract 11), noted on Piper's deed (1796) as "James Craig's corner." The southwest corner of tract 2 was in 1801 the "corner of John Craig and Samuel D. Strain." From the southwest corner of tract 4 (1810) the line ran east along "James Craig's and the Trustees' line" (N of tract 14). The southeast corner of tract 12 was occupied by tract 13, James Craig's donation. From Mitchell's notes it also seems that part of the tract belonged in 1820 or thereabouts to John Taylor. See **Taylor**, and **Bollings Creek**, in Appendix C.

Tract 13. James Craig's donation to the Trustees, 29 November 1796, 5 acres, for a consideration of 5 shillings (DB 5/619). A rectangle adjacent to the southwest corner of tract 14 (Christopher Barbee's donation) and north of tract 21 (Edmond Jones's donation). Only 264 feet wide east to west, and 825 feet long, the land lies athwart present Cameron Avenue in Chapel Hill, west of Pittsboro Street and between that street and Mallette Street, including all the lots on Wilson Street, south of Cameron Avenue. Old maps of Chapel Hill show the tract crossed by the "Avenue" (later Cameron Avenue), with the next road (street) to the south being called "South Street" (today's McCauley Street). The Petersburg road, the "great road," also seems to have crossed the southeast corner of the Craig tract, continuing the southwest direction of the road between tracts 15 and 16. On the deed of 1796, the southeast corner of the Craig tract was designated by a "Post oak near Jones' road"; presumably the same road is the one sometimes designated as the "road to Kittrells."

Tract 14. Christopher Barbee's donation to the trustees, 8 November 1792, 221 acres "on the Chapple Hill," for a consideration of 10 shillings (DB 9/239).

Barbee had bought the land from Hardy Morgan, 12 July 1791 (DB 4/502). This was an L-shaped area, of which the upper (vertical) part is now occupied by downtown Chapel Hill, with its eastern border extending south about to the Old Well on the University campus near Cameron Street, and its west border adjoining the Craig lands (tract 12). On the north it adjoined tracts 4 and 5, partway down the steep hill on present Airport Road. The horizontal bar of the Barbee tract is occupied now by the University campus, extending south approximately to South Road and east to the corner of South Road and Raleigh Street.

Tract 15. Benjamin Yeargain to the trustees, 6 October 1796, 50 acres, for a consideration of 5 shillings (DB 5/616). Yeargain had bought the tract from Hardy Morgan, 25 January 1790 (DB 4/625), when it was described as a part of the "Morgans Chapple Land." The tract was triangular with a sharp southern corner, adjoining Barbee's donation (tract 14) on the east, with a common corner at the south near the Old Well on the present University campus. Its northern boundary, partway down the steep hill on present Airport Road, continued Barbee's line east, approximately to the corner of Boundary Street and North Street. The area is now occupied by most of the "Historic District" of the eastern residential side of Chapel Hill. The somewhat sinuous boundary between this tract and tract 16 followed the northeasterly line of the "great road," the old trade route to "Hallifax and Petersburg."

Tract 16. Hardy Morgan to the trustees, 16 July 1793, 80 acres "on the Chapell Hill adjoining the lands of aforesaid University, the same being part of a larger tract granted by John Erl [*sic*] Granville to Mark Morgan" [on 11 January 1763], for £100 (DB 4/689). The tract adjoins the Barbee lands (tract 14) on its southwest corner, and adjoins land later donated by Hardy Morgan (tract 17) on the southeast. (Although the adjacent tracts 15 and 17 were promised to the trustees in 1792, the deeds were not registered in their name until 1796.) As noted under tract 15, its common boundary with tract 16 follows the "great road," the principal road out to the northeast (for discussion of this old trade route, see above, p. 77). The northern line of tract 16 continues the line of the Barbee and Yeargain donations, east approximately to present Franklin Street as it makes a sweeping curve in the descent to Bolin Creek. The southern edge of the tract essentially parallels Gimghoul Street, extending west to the University campus near Old East. The area includes most of the University Arboretum; Alderman, McIver, and Kenan Dormitories; the Hooper Lane and Senlac Road areas; and Battle Park from Park Place east to the Gimghoul area.

Tract 17. Hardy Morgan to the trustees, 21 October 1796, 125 acres, for a consideration of 5 shillings (DB 5/660). This peculiarly shaped tract adjoins tract 16 (purchased earlier from Morgan) on its northwestern boundaries, and tract 18 (sold by Morgan to John Taylor in 1798 or 1799) on its north and east sides. The northern boundary, as explained in Appendix B, is the boundary between the modern Davie Circle neighborhood and Battle Park, which fortunate coincidence facilitated our work of mapmaking. The southern line of the upper portion of the tract parallels the south side of Gimghoul Road (which is a portion of the road to "Seat [of] Government Wake" shown on the Daniel map of 1792). The southern quadrangle of tract 17 is now occupied mostly by playing fields of the University, south to a little beyond South Road (near the Law School) and thence west to a point northeast of Kenan Stadium, and north along a line at or near Raleigh Street.

Tract 18. Hardy Morgan to John Taylor, proved in court May 1799, 61 3/4 acres for $70 (DB 8/60–61). This is a tract shaped like an inverted L, wrapped around the eastern and northern boundaries of tract 17, with its longer arm running east-west, now occupied by the area of Davie Circle, and its southern boundary adjoining tract 17. The shorter arm is oriented north-south, its eastern boundary near the edge of Battle Park, approximately at Greenwood Road.

Tract 19. Samuel Hopkins to Pleasant Henderson, 15 August 1799, 173 acres (DB 9/289–290). In Carrboro, bounded on the north by tracts 10 and 11, on the east by Greensboro Street and tract 20, and for about 280 feet at the south end by tract 28 (Kittrell's land). The south side was a joint boundary with tract 28. In the deed to tract 19 this and the western boundary-lines were described in terms that seem impossibly vague today, but were acceptably detailed in the unsettled country of 1799. The line ran east-west, 168 poles (about 2772 feet, or more than 1/2 mile) from an oak on the south side of a branch, "to a sugar tree a little above the mouth of a branch and on the North side of Morgan's creek," then the western boundary "up the meanders of said branch" 190 poles (about 3135 feet, or about 0.6 mile) to a willow oak near the head of the branch — i.e., near the southwest corner of tract 10. Another branch bisected tract 19 from the northwest to near its southeast corner, from behind the present Carrboro Town Hall to near the intersection of the Route 54 bypass and Smith Level Road. Present Jones Ferry Road passes near the north end of tract 19 in an ENE–WSW direction from the southern line of Piper's donation (tract 11), and the bypass crosses the south end of the tract.

Tract 20. Edmond Jones to James S. Gillaspie, 24 September 1798, 100 acres "on the Westward side of the village of the University" (DB 8/43). Sold by Gillaspie to Mathew McCauley, 3 October 1799 (DB 10/341), and by McCauley to Joseph Caldwell, 30 October 1805 (DB 12/120). This rectangular tract adjoined tract 19 (at Greensboro Street, Carrboro) on the west, and the "line with the University lands," at or near present Merritt Mill road (tract 21) on the east. It lay between Brewer Lane to the north, "James Craig's line" (tract 12), and the site of present Lincoln School to the south, where it adjoined Bryant Kittrell's property (tract 28). The eastern part of tract 20 was in Chapel Hill, near the site of the present UNC power plant.

Tract 21. Edmond Jones to the trustees, 31 October 1796, 200 acres "on Chappel Hill," for a consideration of 10 shillings (DB 5/668). An L-shaped plot, the large northern quadrangle extending northwest to between present Graham Street and Merritt Mill Road, and now occupied by one of the older residential areas south of the center of Chapel Hill, mostly south and southwest of the University Hospital complex, and including the Westwood and Forest Hills neighborhoods as far south as Merritt's land north of Morgan Creek (tract 30). The east arm of Jones's donation extends into what is now a residential area south of Manning Drive (Victory Village, or more recently Odum Village). The tract includes not only the above, but the modern UNC power plant and most of the McCauley–Ransom Street neighborhood. The southwest continuation of the "great road" from Petersburg, Virginia, seems to have crossed to the WSW, from near the joint corner of tracts 13, 14, and 21.

Tract 22. John and Solomon P. Morgan, the heirs of Mark Morgan, to the trustees, promised 8 November 1792, the deed executed 6 August 1806, 107 acres "near New Hope Chapel," for a consideration of 5 shillings (DB 12/282). An almost exactly square tract, now occupied mostly by the University Hospital complex, its eastern boundary just west of Kenan Stadium. The area extended more or less from present Patterson Place near the intersection with Ransom Street, east to near Kenan Stadium, south beyond the hospital complex and Manning Drive, west to South Columbia Street in the Westwood residential area, and north to the beginning.

Tract 23. John Daniel [Jr.] to the trustees, 18 April 1796, 107 acres "lying partly on New Hope Chapel Hill on both sides of the Rock Springs branch," for a consideration of 5 shillings (DB 5/445). An almost exactly square tract adjoining tract 22 on the east, and said to be of the same acreage, although the stated north-south dimensions of the two tracts differ by an amount of 1/2 pole. The area extends from the present Bell Tower parking lot adjacent to (west of) Kenan Stadium, east to the Law School building on Ridge Road, south to near Hinton James Dormitory on Manning Drive, west to the hospital complex south of Manning Drive, and north to the beginning. In addition to Kenan Stadium, this tract includes Boshamer baseball stadium, and the Ehringhaus, Hinton James, Morrison, and Craige Dormitories.

Tracts 24–27. After the death of Solomon Morgan, his heirs petitioned the Court to rule on the equitable allotment of his real property in southeastern Orange County (DB 33/219–221). The five Commissioners appointed by the Court reported on their decision to the session of November 1848[3]. Four adjoining "lots" numbered 1, 2, 3, and 4, more or less equal in area, and comprising together ca. 1300 acres, were allotted respectively to Sampson Morgan, Mary Morgan, Louisa Morgan, and Jones Morgan. Four additional small contiguous acreages, amounting to ca. 43–45 acres each, in a tract on the Chatham County line to the south of the larger property, were allotted to the same heirs. The lots were surveyed in September 1848, and the original surveyor's descriptions of our tracts 25, 26, and 27, with plats drawn to scale, are in the University of North Carolina Archives, UNC-CH Library. Mary Morgan (later Mrs. James P. Mason) bequeathed to the University the so-called Mason Farm, which in 1894 amounted (according to her estimate) to some 800 acres, she having acquired by purchase or gift the eastern half (amounting to 175 acres) of Louisa Morgan's land, "Lot no. 3," and all but the eastern one-third of "Lot no. 1."

Tract 24. Allotted to Jones Morgan, 325 acres, "Lot no. 4." This adjoined University lands (tracts 17 and 23) lying to its north and west. It covered what is now the area around the Old Chapel Hill Country Club lands between Laurel Hill Road and the Route 54 bypass, the area around the St. Thomas More School, and the Glenwood School and the Highland Woods neighborhood southeast of the bypass.

---

[3]On Solomon Morgan's gravestone in the small cemetery between the clubhouse of the University golf course and the floodplain of Morgan Creek, the date of his death is given as November 17, 1847.

Tract 25. Allotted to Louisa Morgan, 347 acres, "Lot no. 3." This tract adjoined tract 24 on the south, and in a small western extension bordered on University property (tracts 21 and 23). To its south were lands of William Barbee and William Merritt, and to its east was Mary Morgan's property, tract 26. In modern terms it includes the branch and hollow behind Hinton James Dormitory at its west end, and the Meeting of the Waters area just east of Manning Drive. The eastern part of this tract today contains the North Carolina Botanical Garden area and the sewage treatment plant south of Mason Farm Road. Morgan Creek flows in a large loop through its southeast corner. At the partition of Louisa's lands to her heirs in 1857, Jones Morgan inherited the west half of "Lot no. 3."

Tract 26. Allotted to Mary Morgan, 346 acres, "Lot No. 2." This is a long area, lying north-south, that today contains most of Finley Golf Course and Fraternity Row along the north end of Mason Farm Road. It lay between tracts 25 and 27, and was bounded both north and south by lands of William Barbee. The old Morgan (later Mason) farmhouse was located on this tract, very near the present clubhouse for the golf course.

Tract 27. Allotted to Sampson Morgan, 272 acres, "Lot No. 1." This, the eastern part of Solomon Morgan's original property, lies near the eastern limits of modern Chapel Hill, southwest of the intersection of Route 54 and Barbee's Chapel Road, and today includes the site of the University's Friday Center and the Faculty Club, as well as the cleared fields south of Morgan Creek, the site of former research stations and later of town garden-allotments. The western two-thirds of the property, approximately, ultimately became the property of Mary Morgan Mason and her husband, and was bequeathed to the University of North Carolina as part of the Mason Farm.

Tract 28. Edmond Jones to Bryant Kittrell, 7 October 1802, 578 1/2 acres "on both sides of Morgans Creek" (DB 12/103). Southwest of Chapel Hill and south of Carrboro. The tract occupied most of the valley of Morgan Creek, from approximately 0.6 km (ca. 3/8 mile) west of the present crossing of routes 15-501, west to the edge of McCauley's property (near the existing McCauley cemetery), and south into the hills to almost 1 km south of the creek. Part of the western boundary of the tract was formed by the north side of the creek. Most of what was Kittrell's land is now taken up by relatively new residential developments on the outer fringes of Chapel Hill and Carrboro. Kittrell sold the property and some additional acreage to William Durham, 22 November 1832 (DB 29/348).

Tract 29. John Morgan to William Merritt, 25 July, 1787, 50 acres (DB 4/133). A narrow rectangle lying between Kittrell's property (tract 28) and the bulk of Merritt's land (tract 30). The northwest corner is noted as being on "Edmond Jones line" — i.e., the boundary of tract 21, nine years before Jones donated the land to the trustees. Morgan Creek crossed tract 29 near the south end, more or less from northwest to southeast.

Tract 30. Edward [*sic*] Jones to Wm. H. Merritt, 4 March 1807, 338 1/2 acres "on both sides of Morgan's Creek" (DB 13/81). Morgan's Creek in fact traverses the narrow southern third of the property, roughly from west to east, passing through a relatively steep-walled valley from Merritt's mill seat (tract 31, near the crossing of the modern road to Pittsboro), down more than 1 km to where the creek makes a first abrupt turn to the north (at Stillhouse Bottom, on lands now administered by the North Carolina Botanical Garden). The high land on both sides of the creek is now becoming a series of elite residential neighborhoods. To the north Merritt's property extended to abut on University lands (the eastern arm of tract 21, Edmond Jones's donation to the Trustees; or, in modern terms, west of Manning Drive and south of the Hospital complex).

Because the territory was so sparsely inhabited in 1807, the legal description of Merritt's property was based very largely on features of the landscape, including trees, and precise identification of the site in modern terms depends mostly upon matching the information in the deed against the known course of Morgan Creek, the known location of Merritt's mill seat, and the known boundaries of the University lands to the north of tract 30. As an excellent example of the language of deeds of this period, a full transcription is included here:

> Begining on a Hiccory on the South side of Morgans Creek runing thence East thirty three chains & twenty five links to a Beech on a branch; then North crossing Morgans Creek Seventy one chains to a Hiccory a corner of the University lands;[4] thence west with the University line fifty seven chains & twenty five links to a Hiccory William Merritts corner; thence with his line South crossing Morgans Creek, thirty nine chains & Seventy five links to a red Oak, thence East Eight chains & Seventy five links to the bank of said Creek, thence down the meanders of the Creek to a stake a corner of Merritts Mill Seat, thence North with a line of the same five chains to a red Oak, thence East ten chains to Banks Branch, thence down the said Branch to the Mouth, thence down the meanders of Morgans Creek, to a Beech, a corner of the Bank Cabbin tract, thence South twenty six chains & Sixty two links to the begining.

Tract 31. John Morgan to William Merritt, 25 July 1787, 5 acres on Morgan Creek, including a mill seat (DB 4/136). On the north side of Morgan Creek, just downstream from the modern crossing of routes 15-501. It seems somewhat ambiguously located in the deed description, but this is clarified by reading it in connection with the description of tract 30. The directions were to go south along the eastern boundary of tract 29, crossing the creek from north to south, then near the southern end of the boundary line proceed east 8.75 chains (ca. 577.5 feet) to the creek, down the meanders to the corner of the mill seat, then follow the three sides of the mill seat, north 5 chains (330 feet), east 10 chains (660 feet) to Banks Branch, and down the branch to Morgan Creek. The mill was active for many years under several different owners, until it was destroyed and obliterated by the severe flood of August 1924; see **Merritt**, in Appendix C.

Tract 32. Richard Thompson to Elisha Mitchell, 27 November 1839, about 244 acres "on the waters of Tom's Creek" (DB 26/26–27). This tract, not contiguous with the others on the map, is included partly because of Mitchell's association with it, and partly because it provided a means of mapping a portion of the course of the "big road leading from Hillsboro to Chatham," now Old Fayetteville Road,

---

[4]The joint corner of tracts 21 and 25. "William Merritts corner" is the northeast corner of tract 29, which had been Merritt's property since 1787. Banks Branch bordered the mill seat on the east.

which still runs nearly parallel to the west side of Carrboro, from its junction with Old Highway 86 (Hillsborough Street) roughly south-southeast to its junction with Jones Ferry Road near University Lake. The western boundary of Mitchell's tract bordered the road from a point ca. 2000 feet (600 m) north of present highway 54, to a point about 4000 feet (1200 m) south of that highway. From there the boundary ran east about 20 chains (1320 feet, or 400 m) to Tom's Creek near where the creek crosses present Weaver Road, and followed the creek up a short distance (ca. 50 m) in a north-northeasterly direction, before turning north in a zigzag course, crossing present highway 54 near the site of the new (1995) Carrboro Post Office, then north and northeast approximately as far as present Carol Street before turning west toward the "big road." Most of the tract is now part of a residential section of Carrboro, in the triangle between present Hillsborough Street (leading from Carrboro to Hillsborough), and Old Fayetteville Road.

A transcript of Mitchell's original deed is included here, as has been done for the deed of tract 30, and for the same reasons. We have not determined the boundaries of the "lands belonging to the trustees of the University," nor the circumstances under which the University later disposed of them. We were able to locate Mitchell's tract in the first place by the accidental discovery of the exposure of flat rocks mentioned in the deed. These rocks, now mostly covered by vegetation, lie on the west side of Old Fayetteville Road near present Carol Street.

> A tract of land...on the waters of Tom's Creek a branch of Morgan's Creek...being butted & bounded as follows Begining at a wild cherry tree on Tom's creek Weaver's line running thence west two chs. & 30 lks to a hickory thence south six chs. & forty lks to a black oak thence west 17 chs. 31 lks to a stake on the big road leading from Hillsboro to Chatham thence along the said road north 31° west 47 chns to a black oak thence north 17 1/2° west along the same road 22 chns. & 50 lks to a post-oak near the flat rocks thence north 6° west along the said road 23 1/2 chs to a hickory on Herbert Colliers line thence east 12 chns & 70 lks to a white oak in a drain thence south 23 chns & 42 lks to a hickory then east 41 chns along the line of the lands belonging to the trustees of the University to the boundary of the lands belonging to Alexander Stan's heirs then along the line of said lands south 8° east 12 1/2 chns to four post oaks in a drain Weaver's line thence along the meanders of the drain in a southwesterly direction 7 1/2 chs to some Maples thence south 20° east 24 ["chns"(?) blotted out] to a persimmon on the edge of the old field thence south 60° west to Tom's Creek thence along the meanders of the creek two chns. & 84 lks to the beginning.

Tract 33. Thomas Connally [*sic*] to the trustees, 17 October 1796, 107 acres, for a consideration of 5 shillings (DB 5/615). We have not located this tract. The instructions in the deed are to begin at a hickory, thence run east 210 poles to a red oak, north 30 poles to a stake, west 290 poles to a stake, south 136 poles to a stake, east 80 poles to a stake, then north 136 poles to the first station. There are obvious discrepancies in the north-south directions. We have not learned what disposition the University made of the land.

Tract 34. John Hogan to the trustees, 7 November 1792, 200 acres, for a consideration of 5 shillings, proved in court November 1796 (DB 5/616). The

University sold the same tract to Hasten Poe, 6 May 1833 (DB 25/401). We have not located this tract precisely. According to both deeds, it adjoined the land of Stephen Lloyd's orphans on the north, Henry Morris's land on the west, Harry's Mountain on the south, and vacant lands on the east. We presume that "Harry's Mountain" was what now appears on the USGS map as Stony Hill, northeast of Calvander settlement, and that Hogan's tract lay to the north of the hill, east of the old Hillsborough road (now called Old Rte. 86), south of Eubanks Road and west of Rogers Road.

Tract 35. Mathew McCauley to the trustees, 7 November 1792, 150 acres, for a consideration of 5 shillings (paid to the Commissioners on the above date, but the deed not proved in court until November 1796) (DB 5/617). The University sold the same tract on 6 March 1833, to James Long (DB 25/428). We have not located this tract, except that it was presumably on the waters of Bolin Creek, northwest of Chapel Hill. The description of the property, which was a rectangle 205 poles long on the northern and southern lines, and 117 poles wide on the eastern and western lines, locates it merely by saying that the northern and eastern boundaries adjoined the property of Thomas Lloyd. James Vickers (1985, page 19), perhaps confusing it with tract 1, states that it comprised 100 acres on Mt. Bolus, but the measurements indicate that the area was approximately 150 acres.

APPENDIX E
THE NUMBERED LOTS IN THE VILLAGE OF CHAPEL HILL (MAP 2)

As noted above (Appendix A), the University Trustees held an auction, advertised for October 12, 1793, offering for sale a total of twenty-four lots of 2 acres each, and six lots of 4 acres each. The auction was discussed by Battle (1907, pp. 44–47), who included the names of twenty-two purchasers and the amount paid by each one, but cited only twelve lots by number.[1] Most of the lots sold at once, but as also noted above, some were not immediately developed. Battle opined that "nearly of all these purchases were for speculative purposes" (1907, p. 47), and this seems to have been true, judging by the quick turnover of many of them. Some remained in the possession of the original owners or their heirs for many years, but others, especially in what became the central part of the "Village of the University," were sold and resold, often after subdivision, some eventually reverting to the Trustees. We have not attempted here to follow all the complicated history of each lot, but have tried to present enough of the picture to show something of the extent of the active trading in real estate, and of what the village was like at the time of Elisha Mitchell's most active interest in the physical features and the vegetation of the village itself and its immediate surroundings (i.e., ca. 1818–1824). In the descriptions of the lots we have tried to include as a minimum the names of the original purchaser or the owner (or owners) about 1820. Also included is the date of purchase and the volume and page of the Deed Book where each transaction is recorded in the office of the Register of Deeds at

---

[1] There are several seeming inconsistencies in Battle's list. Three of the purchasers that he named — viz., Ephraim Frazier, Stephen Gapins, and Lewis Kirk — were all residents of Orange County at the time, but their names seem not to be listed in the Deed Books in connection with this sale. Perhaps they were involved with 2-acre lots 1, 2, 3, or 23, for which we have not found records of sale in 1793. Battle does not mention John W. Carr, who bought lot 7 at the auction, nor (as an original buyer) William Henry Hill, who bought lot 18. Battle also credits Edmund Jones with buying lot 13, when in fact he bought 4-acre lot I. There also seems to be confusion about lots 17 and 18: Battle credits Charles Collier with having paid £67 at the auction, and says the "Charles Collier lot is that at the corner of Hillsboro and Franklin street, now owned by the heirs of Henry Thompson"; this is apparently lot 18, sold by the Trustees in 1793 to William Henry Hill and coming eventually (in 1850) to William Thompson. We find no reference in the deeds to any purchase by Collier until he bought lot 17 from the Trustees in 1803; this is apparently the lot that Battle says was "bid off" by Alfred Moore in 1793, and came eventually into the hands of Thomas Taylor, via William H. Hill, the "land east of the Episcopal church extending to the Raleigh road" (Battle, 1907, p. 46).

Hillsborough. For the benefit of those who are interested in the history of any particular lot, or in the history of old Chapel Hill in general, the text includes brief citations, by volume and page (e.g., "DB 32/436"), to other transactions involving the same property that have come to our attention. We have searched the records systematically, and we have combined our finds with those of Charles Blake (Chapel Hill Historical Society papers). We have also checked our findings with *Orange County Records* (ed. William Doub Bennett), vols. 8 (1991), 11 (1993), 12 (1993), 14 (1994), and 15 (1995), which provide detailed summaries of the contents, respectively, of Deed Books 5, 6 and 7, 8 and 9, 10 and 11, and 12. But we do not pretend that our list is an exhaustive one.

In the following text (intended to be read in conjunction with Map 2), modern references to "the avenue leading to the principal building" are to what is now called Cameron Avenue (the "principal building" was Old East, dating from 1793), and the "public square" is the university campus (or "compass," as it was often spelled). The term "Main Street" is sometimes used when Franklin Street is meant, and "Back Street" was an acceptable name for Rosemary Street down into the twentieth century. The "Grand Avenue" was laid out in the original plan of the village and the campus as a strip 290 feet wide (Battle, 1907, p. 44), the distance bewween the eastern side of the East Building and the western side of the West Building (Old East and Old West), extending northward from the north side of the Main Building (Old South) and providing a grand vista in that direction. As Henderson comments (1949, p. 53), the "Avenue" was never intended to be a thoroughfare, but what today would be called a park. The old Chapel (Person Hall) was located on the west side of the Grand Avenue. Before 1820 the avenue itself was beginning to be constrained and narrowed by development (see map 2).

In Mitchell's early years at the University, the central part of the village was well occupied, and there was considerable traffic in village property, for both private and commercial use. Except for outlying homes of some large landholders, the village itself was confined to the small area shown in Map 2. By 1820 there was still little but woods west of Columbia Street, and only scattered houses to the east of Hillsborough Street. In our descriptions of the lots we refer to street-directions as north, south, east, and west, as do most of the deeds, and we use the modern names, as in "West Franklin Street." As has been mentioned, Franklin and Rosemary Streets were laid out, and remain, more or less on an ENE–WSW axis (at that time N 62° E–S 62° W), and some of the deeds reflect this, albeit imprecisely, as in describing a lot with its "South East" side on Franklin Street and its "North West" side on Rosemary Street. Several of the lots in the more congested part of the village were divided into halves or smaller portions sold separately, and the deeds frequently refer to the "upper" half, surely an ambiguous term on nearly level terrain; at least once reference is made to "the western or upper half of Lott 10," but we have found no consistent usage to clarify the meaning of "upper" in this sense.

The 2-Acre Lots, nos. 1–24

Lot 1 [Northwest of the intersection of Cameron and Columbia Streets]. It seems likely that the original purchaser was Lewis Kirk, who owned land in western Orange County. Battle (1907, p. 46) says that Kirk spent £58 at the auction, but we find no other record of this. He bequeathed the lot (1808; Will Book D/290) to his son James Kirk. James Kirk (31 Mar 1814; DB 15/368) transferred his estate, presumably including lot 1, to John L. Kirk. John Kirk (5 Jul 1817; DB 16/201) sold to James Ward. James Ward (15 Feb 1819; DB 18/194) sold "the same Two Acre Lot that said James Ward bought of John Kirk" to William Barbee and Nathaniel J. King. [The record seems to show that Ward, two months later (28 Apr 1819; DB 17/304) sold what was apparently part of the same property (one and one-half acres) to Pleasant Henderson, a lot "in the Village of Chapel Hill on Columbia Street and Numbered One in the plan of said Village."]

J. Caldwell and Nathaniel J. King (7 Jan 1824; DB 21/132–133) sold to John McGee and John Smith half of what is described as 4-acre "lot no. 1" [evidently in fact the 2-acre lot], previously owned by James Ward, and bounded "on the West by [blank] Street on the South by the avenue leading to the principal building." John McGee (22 Feb 1828; DB 23/137) sold to John Hutchins the same lot, bounded "on the South by the avenue leading to the principal building." McGee found it difficult to meet his obligations on the lot, and signed it over to John Hutchins, who in turn transferred (1 Jun 1829; DB 23/513–515) to Rodman N. Stone, "the House and Lot heretofore owned and occupied by James Ward and bounded on the West by a street and the property of Miss Eliz. Nunn on the south by the avenue leading to the principal Buildings of the University on the East by a street and on the North by the prope[r]ty of N. I. King and the lands of the trustees."

It appears that in 1829 or before, lot 1 was subdivided, but we have not substantiated this, nor have we learned how the property came into the possession of John Lewis; but Rodman Stone (28 Dec 1830; DB 24/225), said in other contemporary deeds to be from New York City, sold a part of the lot, supposedly formerly property of John Lewis, to Orrin [also spelled Oran, Orran, Orren, or Orlan] Lewis. On 27 May 1834 (DB 26/49) Orrin Lewis sold to Elisha Mitchell one and one-half acres (the lot number not specified), including "the MacGee house at present occupied by Mrs. Hargis." According to the description in the deed, the lot lies on the east side of a street (presumably Columbia Street), and the north side of another street (i.e., today's Cameron Avenue). The southwest corner of the lot has been cut out ("South along [Columbia] street to the corner of O. Lewis lot by his wife Elizabeth known as Andersons corner thence East to the corner of his Garden then South to the Street"). The northeast corner has been cut out, and is the property of Nathaniel I. King. The north boundary is said to adjoin "a lot now known as the Bottonickal Garden"; we surmise that the "Bottonickal Garden" is 2-acre lot 3, for which we have no other record.

Map 2. The village lots offered for sale by the University trustees, October 14–19, 1793. From a "Plan of the Village of Chapel Hill," with date of Sept. 4, 1817, "Copy from a Plot in the possession of Wm Pannill which was taken from the Plot of John Craig Esq." Original in the North Carolina Collection, University of North Carolina Library at Chapel Hill: used with permission. For description and discussions of individual lots, see the text of this Appendix.

The rectangular boundaries above and to the right and left of the village are the boundaries of the University property at the time, all the lines directed E-W or N-S. The western boundary of the property, just outside village lot No. 7, is also the western boundary of tract No. 14 on our map No. 1 (Christopher Barbee's donation to the Trustees), with a step-like projection indicating the position of tract No. 13 (James Craig's donation).

On this map, the Grand Avenue (98 feet wide according to the caption on the original plat) lies between 4-acre lots III and IV and extends southeast towards the buildings of the University, crossed first by Rosemary and then by Franklin Streets. Columbia Street starts at Rosemary Street between 2-acre lots 7 and 8 and ends at 4-acre lots I and II.

Lots in the village

Fig. 2. The "President's House," Elisha Mitchell's home for most of his career in Chapel Hill, as it looked in 1906. Photograph by Collier Cobb, published by courtesy of the North Carolina Collection, University of North Carolina Library at Chapel Hill.

Lot 2 [The "President's Lot," east of 2-acre lot 1, at the southwest corner of the "Campus," north of the Avenue and east of Columbia Street]. Elisha Mitchell lived in the "President's House" on this lot for most of his years at the University. We have no information as to the original purchaser; perhaps it remained in the hands of the Trustees.

Lot 3 [North of 2-acre lot 1, west side of Columbia Street]. We have no information as to the original purchaser, or any subsequent buyer, but see a note above under Lot 1.

Lot 4 [East of lot 3, across Columbia Street]. The Trustees (17 Oct 1793; DB 5/85) sold to James Patterson, by two separate deeds, lots 4 and 5, for £47 10s and £61, respectively. Patterson (13 Oct 1795; DB 5/265) sold both lots to William Nunn. Nunn (in 1805; see Lot 6 for details) combines lots 4 and 6. Henderson (1949, p. 55) mentions the "inn which is believed to have stood there in Revolutionary days," which William Nunn and his wife Elizabeth presumably had in mind when buying the property, as William at once began to advertise "that he is now living at the University of North Carolina, and keeps a house of Entertainment."

Lot 5 [Northwest of lot 4, across and on the west side of Columbia Street and the south side of Franklin Street]. For transfers to James Patterson and William Nunn (1793, 1795), see Lot 4.

Lot 6 [East of lot 5, southeast of the intersection of Columbia and Franklin Streets, and north of lot 4]. We find no record of this, but the Trustees (1793) presumably sold lot 6 to Archibald Campbell, who paid £54 10s for a lot at the auction (Battle, 1907, p. 46). Campbell sold lot 6 (27 Aug 1797; DB 9/168) to

William Nunn, who had owned the adjoining lot 4 since 1795. Nunn (22 Nov 1805; DB 12/89) combined lots 4 and 6 into a single tract, and sold (or gave) the eastern half, south from the "Main Street" to the president's lot [= lot 2], "thence East to the publick Square" and north to the beginning, to his son David H. Nunn. David Nunn (11 Nov 1809; DB 22/404) sold to Elias Haw[e]s. Haw[e]s (27 Apr 1814; DB 19/247) sold to William Barbee.

Lot 7 [Northwest of the intersection of Franklin and Columbia Streets, and occupying the entire block north to Rosemary Street]. The Trustees (5 Oct 1846; DB 32/221) sold to John W. Carr lot 7 "on the side of Fayetteville [Columbia] Street opposite to the residence of Mrs. Nunn."

Lot 8 [East of Columbia Street, between Franklin and Rosemary Streets]. The Trustees (17 Oct 1793; DB 6/9) sold it to John Carrington, Sr., for £52. James Carrington, "Jr.," (30 Nov 1797 according to the deed; DB 6/235) acquired the lot by sheriff's sale, and sold it (perhaps the same day, but according to the deed 13 Nov 1797; DB 6/376) to Matthew McCauley. McCauley (29 Apr 1819; DB 20/41) sold to Joseph Thompson 600 square feet in the southeast corner. William [sic] McCauley (19 Apr 1822; DB 20/417) sold [Dr.] Charles R. Yancey lot 8 (apparently except for the same 600 square feet, "Twenty feet in front & Thirty feet back at the Eastern Corner of said lot adjoining Franklin Street which James Thompson & George Trice heretofore purchased from Matthew McCauley and upon which they erected a Store House"). "Yancy" (27 Jan 1824; DB 21/ 305–306) sold Christopher Barbee, Sr., part of lot 8, ca. 0.7 acre, apparently a rectangle in the southwest corner, with 33 feet of frontage on Franklin Street, between Barbee's existing blacksmith shop and the corner of Columbia Street, and 56 feet of frontage on the latter.

Lot 9 [South side of Franklin Street, between lots 6 and 11]. The Trustees (17 Oct 1793; DB 6/8) sold it to John Carrington (who also bought lot 8; see above), for £55. His son James Carrington, "Jr." (30 May 1797; DB 7/215) sold it to John McCauley. The lot was divided into [eastern and western] halves. McCauley (31 May 1798; DB 7/213–214) sold to John Caldwell one half of the lot. The description of the property portrays vividly some of the frontier surroundings then existing in what is now downtown Chapel Hill: "adjoining the lot formerly purchased by Alexdr Mebane on the West and adjoining the other half of said lot on the East. Begining at Mebane's lower corner on Franklin Street Runing South with the line of said lot to the South East corner of Mebane said lot near to an old saw pit thence East with the line of said Lot as far as will be sufficient to make or include one half of said two acre lot to a stake thence North a long a line of Chopped Trees to a stake on Franklin Street so as to divide the said two acre lot Number Nine (9) Exactly in two thence west with Franklin Street to the begining." We find no other record of Alexander Mebane's ownership of this property.

John Caldwell (28 Sep 1803; DB 11/242) sold to Thomas Edwards half of lot 9, presumably the same half, described as lying between the lot of William Nunn [lot 6] and that of John McCauley [lot 11]. Certainly the same half, "bounded on the north by Franklin Street," was sold by the sheriff (execution on Thomas Edwards, 24 Aug 1807; DB 13/31) to David Nunn. We have no information as to how the lot eventually evolved into University campus. For transactions in 1841 and 1843, see DB 29/468, 30/372, 31/10.

Lot 10 [between Franklin and Rosemary Streets, east of lot 8 and west of lot 12]. The Trustees (18 Oct 1793; DB 5/600) sold it to Daniel Booth for £52. By 1806 it was in the hands of John Dixon [in 1810 called Joseph Dixon] and John Adams, who (31 Jul 1806; DB 12/343) sold to Whitted & Craig half of lot 10, "formerly the property of Daniel Boothe," and "bounded on the North East [East] by half of said lot" ["Adams's half of the original Lott," ex DB 14/28], "on South East [South] by Franklin Street on the South west [West, lot 8] by Matthew McCauley and on the North west [North] by a street [Rosemary] it being the western or upper half of Lott No 10." The same property, when sold by Edward Robson (21 Sep 1810; DB 13/623) to Joseph Caldwell and Pleasant Henderson, was described as bounded on the northwest by McCauley's lot, on the southwest and northeast each by a street, and on the fourth side by part of the same lot belonging to John Adams. [William] Whitted and [John] Craig (25 Jul 1810; DB 14/27–28) had sold to James Putney one acre, "being the South West half of a Two acre lott...(No. 10)." Edward Robson (18 Sep 1816; DB 17/214) sold to Thomas H. Taylor lot 10, "bounded on the North side by a back Street or lane, on the South Side by the North side of Franklin Street and on the other sides of said Lot, by the Lots owned by Mathew McCawley and Major Pleasant Henderson, being the said Lot on which the said Robson kept store and now keeps the Post Office," except that portion which "Robson has heretofore sold and conveyed to Edmund Pitt & Nathaniel King (merchants)." On 21 Feb 1817 (DB 16/38) Robson sold to Edmund Pitt [sic! but in DB 24/184 he is called Edward R. Pitt] a part of lot 10, "Begining at the South East corner of the upper half of Lot Number Ten (10) now the property of Thomas Taylor and on which he now lives and runing along Franklin Street Forty feet in front of the other half of lot 10 and thence back of Franklin Street at right angles one hundred & forty four feet it being the upper corner of the half of the lot conveyed to said Robson by John Adams bounded on the East & North sides by the balance of said lot."

Thomas H. Taylor (4 Sep 1817; DB 16/163) sold to Abraham Craig the part of lot 10 "which I lately purchased of Edward Robson saving & excepting" the part bought by Edward [sic] Pitt from Robson "previous to my purchase," bounded "on the North side by a back street or lane, on the South side by Franklin Street on the East side by Pleasant Henderson & on the West by McCawley & Thompsons Ground."

Pitt (8 Jun 1821; DB 24/184) sold to John A. Ramsay the part of lot 10 that Robson had sold to Pitt in 1817, and the "heirs of John Ramsay" (28 Jun 1824; DB 21/308), by sheriff's sale, transferred it to Benjamin Rhodes [see also DB 23/118–119, 14 Jan (1828), for exactly the same description of a lot sold by Benjamin Rhodes to Daniel Boothe]; and Daniel Booth (3 Jul 1830; DB 24/184) sold Jesse Mason the upper half of lot 10. On 16 Jul 1831 (DB 26/258) Jesse Mason sold Daniel Boothe a parcel "Begining at the South East corner of the upper half of lot No. ten (10),...running thence along Franklin Street forty five feet in front of the other half Lot No. Ten (10) thence back of Franklin Street at angles one hundred & forty five feet the same being the half of Lot No. 10 heretofore sold by Edward Robson to Edward R. Pitt" (in 1817).

Pleasant Henderson (20 Apr 1822; DB 20/66) sold to Benjamin Rhodes one acre of lot 10, its western half, "with the houses thereon." Subsequently (8 Oct 1828; DB 23/381), a sheriff's sale transferred (from John McGee) to Dr. James Webb of Hillsborough a part of lot 10 comprising one acre on Franklin Street, "occupied by John Hutchens, Anderson Blackwood & Co. & Jane Craig"; the property was "bounded East by Daniel Boothe — West by Dr. Charles R. Yancy." James Webb (17 Oct 1832; DB 25/244) sold to John Hutchens a part of lot 10 "now occupied by John Hutchens and others."

See also DB 23/471, 23/478, 24/225, 1829–1830, for sales involving one-quarter acre formerly belonging to John Lewis. Note the apparent duplication under lots 12 and 14, with several different small lots.

Lot 11 [South side of Franklin Street, east of lot 9, west side of the Grand Avenue]. The Trustees (16 Oct 1793; DB 5/84) sold it to George Johnston for £71; shortly thereafter, Johnston (25 Feb 1794; DB 5/123) sold it to John McCauley. McCauley (18 Apr 1796; DB 5/667) sold back to the Trustees a 60-foot strip along the east side (i.e., next to the Grand Avenue). McCauley (15 Apr 1804; DB 11/186) sold to William Richardson Davie a part of lot 11, "bounded on the East by the great Avenue begining at the corner of the Store house of the said McCauley where the said Street intersects the great Avenue and runing westwardly with the said Street One hundred and fifty one feet thence by a line runing at right angles...southwardly to the publick ground," thence east and north to complete the rectangle. (This strip of 151 feet, added to the 60-foot strip sold to the Trustees in 1796, would amount to about half of the 2-acre lot).

James Hogg (22 Jul 1808; DB 13/155) sold William Norwood property, "Begining at the corner of the Store house now occupied by the said James Hogg where the said [Franklin] Street intersects the grand Avenue and runing thence westwardly with the said Street one hundred and fifty one feet, thence by a line runing at right angles...southwesterly to the public grounds, thence eastwardly one hundred and fifty one 151 feet to the South East corner of said Lott, thence down the Grand Avenue to the first Station." We have no information on how this property came into Hogg's hands. For subsequent history of this lot (1832–1846), including the western part, see DB 28/8, 29/231, 30/227, 31/157, 32/30, 33/37.

Lot 12 [East of lot 10, west of the Grand Avenue, between Franklin and Rosemary Streets]. The Trustees (17 Oct 1793; DB 5/83–84) sold it to Hardy Morgan for £75, and Morgan (1 Sep 1794; DB 5/226) soon sold it to Samuel Hopkins. Pleasant Henderson moved to Chapel Hill (according to Henderson, 1949, pp. 56–57) with his family in 1797 and "built a spacious dwelling on the site of the present U.S. Post Office, together with a store on the same lot"; Henderson presumably bought the lot soon after his arrival, but we have not verified this. N. I. King (1 Sep 1839; DB 30/108), as agent for Alexander Henderson of Mobile, sold to Anna Ashe approximately seven-eighths of an acre, a lot "on the main street in Chapel Hill late the residence of Maj. Pleasant Henderson beginning at the East corner of said lot & runing with the main street South 38 West one hundred twelve (112) feet to a stake on Franklin Street, runing thence a direct line a distance of Two Hundred Ninety six feet to the Back Street [i.e. Rosemary Street], then with the Back Street North 62 East One hundred and twelve feet to the cross street, dividing the said lot from the lot on which the village Chapel is situated, then with said Cross Street to the beginning." Anna L. Ashe subsequently sold the lot (17 Jul 1867; DB 42/62) to Andrew Mickle, at which time the "cross street," as carved out of the Grand Avenue, is identified under its present name of Henderson Street.

Lot 13 [South of Franklin Street and east of the Grand Avenue]. The Trustees (14 Oct 1793; DB 5/209) sold it to Jesse Nevill for £76 10s. (Battle, 1907, p. 46, says that Edmund Jones bought lot 13.) Nevell [sic] (22 Aug 1796; DB 5/590) sold the lot to John Taylor. We have not followed the subsequent history of the lot; much of it is now University property.

Lot 14 [Between Franklin and Rosemary Streets, east of the Grand Avenue]. The Trustees (18 Oct 1793; DB 5/57) sold it to Samuel Hopkins for £33, "currency of North Carolina." The lot was almost at once subdivided. Hopkins sold (24 Nov 1794; DB 5/245) to John Kimble a part, probably the northwest corner, consisting of one-half acre; he then sold (22 Aug 1796; DB 5/491) to William Henry Haywood probably the southwest half-acre. Haywood (19 Oct 1812; DB 14/345) sold to John Taylor, Sr., the half of lot 14 he had bought from Hopkins. John Taylor, Sr. (28 Jun 1814; DB 14/724) sold to Thomas H. Taylor "one half acre of lot 14, to include the South West corner and one-sixth acre adjoining that half acre on the East side runing on the line of the main Street and on the line of the Avenue," originally purchased from William H. Haywood. Thomas Taylor (28 Jun 1831; DB 24/460) sold to Walter Norwood a part of lot 14, "Beginning at South West corner of my shoe shop so as to include said shop on Franklin Street, thence a strait line nearly North to Blake's line, thence East with said line, thence nearly South to Franklin Street thence West...to the beginning." We have not identified the Blake mentioned in this deed.

Archibald Reeves (15 Nov 1813; DB 18/15) sold to Edmund [sic] R. Pitt "between one acre and three-quarters...the eastern part and Residue of the Lot claimed by Taylor" and known as lot 14, "bounded by said Taylor on the West and on the East by a Two Acre Lot claimed by [Robert] Campbell" (i.e., lot 16, which was indeed owned by Campbell until 1819). Reeves had purchased (2 Mar 1801; DB 9/286) this property from James Mitchell, who had acquired it by sheriff's sale, at a time when Bennett Watson was said to be occupying it.

William Whitted (17 Sep 1811; DB 14/26) sold to Thomas H. Taylor lot 14, "beginning at the North corner of the House...and thence along William H. Haywood's line to the Avenue, it being the West corner of the lott bought...of Joseph Stubbins who bought of Bennett Watson and he bought of Samuel Hopkins." This is evidently the same property sold by George "Nuting" (27 Jun 1801; DB 10/88) to Joseph Stubbins, Jr., the northwest corner of a 2-acre lot: from the east end of the dwelling house on the back street, south to Haywood's line, west with his line to the avenue, north with the avenue to the back street, and east with the street to the beginning.

Items in DB 23/478 (sheriff to Rodman N. Stone) and 24/225 (Stone to Orrin Lewis) are apparently duplicated under lots 10 and 14 (23/478) and under lot 16 (24/225), but each refers to a different small lot.

Lot 15 [South side of Franklin Street, between lots 13 and 17]. According to Battle (1907, p. 46), Nathaniel Christmas paid £40 for property at the auction of 1793. We have found no record of the transaction among the deeds, but Christmas did subsequently (10 Oct 1797; DB 6/372) sell lot 15 to Augustus [Augustine] Benton; Benton (3 Dec 1806; DB 12/333) sold it to his father-in-law, John Taylor, Sr., for £50. On 17 Dec 1824 the lot sold at a sheriff's sale to John's son, Thomas H. Taylor, for $99. The Chapel of the Cross now occupies a tract between lots 15 and 17, including portions taken from each.

Lot 16 [Between Franklin Street and Rosemary Street, between lots 14 and 18]. The Trustees (18 Oct 1793; DB 5/164) sold it to John Daniel for £28. Daniel (16 Oct 1797; DB 6/230) sold the western half of the lot to Robert Campbell, and later (16 Aug 1799; DB 8/190) the eastern half to Campbell as well. Campbell (15 Mar 1819; DB 19/115) sold the entire lot to George W. Trice, and George (7 May 1819; DB 18/99) sold it to Harrison Trice. William and Harrison Trice (28 Feb 1824; DB 20/449–451) divided the lot by two lines from Franklin Street to Rosemary Street, William taking an acre in the center and Harrison the two half-acre tracts adjoining lots 14 and 18. For subsequent developments see DB 23/182, 23/478, 24/225, 26/49.

Lot 17 [East of lot 15, southwest of the intersection of Franklin and Hillsborough/Raleigh Streets]. Battle (1907, p. 46) says that at the auction in 1793 this lot was bid in for £32 by Alfred Moore, who was one of the Commissioners, and that Moore transferred the deed to William H. Hill, who in turn transferred it to Thomas H. Taylor. The facts are apparently somewhat different; Hill seems instead to have bought lot 18 (which see). We have no information about the early history of the lot until 20 May 1803, when the the Trustees (DB 11/157) sold it to Charles Collier for £75. Collier endorsed the deed to Augustus [Augustine] Benton, and he to his mother, Frances Benton (5 Aug 1803; DB 11/118). Frances Benton (27 Jul 1814; DB 14/725) sold to Augustine's brother-in-law, Thomas H. Taylor. According to Battle, Taylor built a house on this lot and lived on it, but he eventually (13 Aug 1835; DB 29/509) sold it to the Trustees. See Lot 15 for a note on the eventual disposition of the western part of this lot.

Lot 18 [Between Franklin and Rosemary Streets, east of lot 16, west side of Hillsborough Street]. The Trustees (18 Oct 1793; DB 5/33) sold it to William Henry Hill for £32 ("32 Curency"). Hill (7 Jul 1804; DB 12/227) sold to John Taylor, Sr. The lot was conveyed by sheriff's sale (17 Dec 1824; DB 21/425) to Thomas H. Taylor, who sold it (29 Jan 1825; DB 21/490) to William "White." Thomas E. "Whyte" (17 Jun 1850; DB 37/517) sold it to William Thompson.

Lot 19 [Southeast of the intersection of Franklin Street and Raleigh Street, adjoining lot 21]. The Trustees (18 Oct 1793; DB 5/58–59) sold it to John Grant Rencher, who bought at the same time lot 20, and 4-acre lot V. He paid £77 for the two 2-acre lots together. Rencher (16 Apr 1798; DB 7/38) sold lot 19 to Joseph Caldwell. For its subsequent history, see Lot 21.

Lot 20 [East side of Hillsborough Street, between Franklin and Rosemary Streets]. The Trustees (18 Oct 1793; DB 5/59) sold it to John Rencher. Rencher (14 Aug 1799; DB 8/183) sold to Augustus [Augustine] Benton; Benton (4 Dec 1806; DB 22/403) sold to Frederick Collier. Collier (14 Nov 1809; DB 22/404) sold 2 acres to Elias Haws [Hawes] as two lots of "ground" on Franklin Street and "known as number 20," and Hawes (13 May 1831; DB 25/113) sold the same "2 lots" to James Phillips.

Lot 21 [South side of Franklin Street, between lots 19 and 23]. The Trustees (17 Oct 1793; DB 5/179) sold it to Chesley Page Patterson, who bought this and lot 22 at the same time, the two together for £82. We find no record of when Patterson parted with lot 21, but it was acquired before 1819, along with lot 23, by

Joseph Caldwell, who already owned lot 19. Caldwell (21 May 1819; DB 17/362–363) sold (really gave, for the sum of $10) to William Hooper about half of lot 21 (the eastern half next to lot 23) and all of lot 23. When President Caldwell died in 1835, he willed (Will Book E/363) lot 19 and his half of lot 21 to William Hooper, who sold the same (15 Jan 1838; DB 29/115) to the Trustees, the property then said to consist of a rectangle with 382 feet of frontage on Franklin Street, and a depth of 296 feet. William Hooper subsequently (2 Sep 1839; DB 32/31–33) conveyed to his son John de Berniere Hooper the property he himself had received from Caldwell in 1819 (i.e., lot 23 and about half of lot 21). The same property was owned by a University professor, Manuel Fetter, from 1850 to 1870 (DB 33/538, 40/160).

Lot 22 [North of lot 21, between Franklin and Rosemary Streets]. The Trustees (17 Oct 1793; DB 5/179) sold it to Chesley Page Patterson (also lot 21, directly opposite, on the south side of Franklin Street). Patterson (2 Oct 1810; DB 13/467) sold the western half of the lot to Edward Robson. Robson (6 Feb 1815; DB 16/23–24) sold to John Craig the same half of lot 22, "on the North side of Franklin Street," bounded on the west by the lot of Dr. Elias Hawes "& on the East by the other side of said lot." John Craig (Feb 1817; DB 15/438) sold the same to Jane Puckett; she sold it (Jun 1820; DB 18/335) to Denison Olmsted; and he (1 Sep 1822; DB 21/244) sold it to the university Trustees.

We find no record of when William Hooper acquired the eastern half of lot 22, but on 23 Jan 1838 (DB 32/294) he sold it to James Phillips, bounded "on the West by one half of lot No. 22...(now occupied by the said James Phillips)...on the East by a lot belonging to [blank]...it being the eastern half of said lot No. 22."

Lot 23 [At the eastern boundary of Chapel Hill, south side of Franklin Street, east of lot 21]. This was apparently not sold by the Trustees at the original auction. It was owned at one time by Joseph Caldwell and later by William Hooper and John de Berniere Hooper, the latter of whom (14 Oct 1850; DB 33/538) sold it and a part of lot 21 to Manuel Fetter. For details see Lot 21.

Lot 24 [At the eastern boundary of Chapel Hill, between Franklin and Rosemary Streets, east of lot 22]. The Trustees (19 Oct 1793; DB 6/321) sold it for £29 to John Caldwell. The lot was sold by the sheriff (20 May 1815; DB 17/359) to James Child, and assigned to Thomas Hatch. It was subsequently divided. Hatch (8 Apr 1819; DB 17/359) sold the eastern half to William Mason, described as one acre on the north side of the main street where John Caldwell formerly lived and the most easterly lot in the plan of the said village. Mason (25 Feb 1835; DB 27/80) sold it to Abijah Hatch, who sold it (8 Nov 1848; DB 54/136) to Charles Phillips.

The western half of lot 24 seems to have been owned by the Trustees on 5 Mar 1847, when they sold (DB 32/512) to William M. Green one acre, from the southeast corner of Prof. [James] Phillips' ["formerly J. J. Collier's"] lot, along Franklin Street 148 feet to Abijah Hatch's southwest corner (i.e., the corner of lot 24, eastern half, which Abijah Hatch acquired in 1835 and sold in 1848), thence with Hatch's line 296 feet to the back street. The reference to the Collier lot — actually lot 20 — seems to have been an error on the part of the Court; James Phillips acquired lot 20 in 1831, but he had also acquired the eastern half of lot 22 in 1838.

W. M. Green (23 Nov 1850; DB 33/529) sold what is surely the same tract as the above to Charles Phillips, the deed locating it between a lot owned by James Phillips on the west and a lot owned by the said Charles Phillips on the east, the last being the last lot upon that side of the street according to the plan of the village before 1840 (i.e., the eastern half of lot 24, acquired by Charles Phillips in 1848).

The 4-Acre Lots, nos. I–VI

Lot I [South of 2-acre lot 2, south of the "avenue leading to the principal buildings" and southeast of the end of Columbia Street]. The Trustees (19 Oct 1793; DB 5/196–197) sold it to Edmund Jones for £100, "currency of North Carolina." Jones (23 Jul 1799; DB 8/142) sold (for the sum of £77 10s) to James L. Gillaspie "lot 1," "on the South side of the Avenue leading from the publick buildings of the University by the Presidents house" (which is on 2-acre lot 2). Gillaspie (14 Oct 1799; DB 9/4) sold to William Edwards Webb; Webb (22 Apr 1817; DB 21/563) sold the western half of the lot to William Pannill; Webb also (3 Mar 1819; DB 18/70) sold half (presumably the eastern half) of the lot to Lucy Hilliard. Lucy "Hillyard" (29 Oct 1819; DB 18/71) sold to Elisha Mitchell half of lot I, "divided by a right line paralel to the Eastern line of Lot number Two...and also paralel to the line of Lot number one" (i.e., a north-south division). William Pannill (31 Jan 1820; DB 18/18) sold to William Hooper the [western] half, "the other half now belonging to [Lucy] Hillyard. "

Lot II [West of and adjoining 4-acre lot I, south of the end of Columbia Street at its intersection with the Avenue (now Cameron Avenue)]. The Trustees (19 Oct 1793; DB 6/438) sold it to Christopher Barbee for £105 10s. Barbee (19 Feb 1798; DB 6/461) sold to Samuel Allen Holmes. Holmes (22 Jun 1799; DB 8/185) sold to William Edwards Webb. Webb (27 Apr 1817; DB 21/563) sold to William Pannill lot II, and the western half of lot I (see also under Lot I, above). Subsequently its history becomes more difficult to interpret. Pannill (5 Dec 1818; DB 17/310) sold to Elisha Mitchell one-half (presumably the eastern half) of lot II, and half "of one adjoining"; but the western half of lot I Pannill sold again, this time to William Hooper in 1820, with no other lot "adjoining," and he also (29 Aug 1825; DB 21/538) sold to John Lewis one-half of "lot 1" and one-half of "lot 2," 4 acres more or less, and part of the lot sold by William E. Webb to Pannill on "27 [sic] April 1817"; John Lewis (21 Mar 1828; DB 23/277) sold the same 4-acre combined lot to N. I. King]. For the western half of lot II, see also DB 21/359, 21/538, 21/539, 21/545, 21/551, 32/503.

Lot III [North side of Rosemary Street, west side of the Grand Avenue, extending north approximately to the line of present North Street]. The Trustees (19 Oct 1793; DB 5/95) sold this lot of 4 acres, "called a square," for £50, to Andrew Burk[e], a Hillsborough merchant (he bought 4-acre lot VI at the same time). Burke (11 Apr 1795; DB 5/253) sold it to Lemuel (Samuel?) Robinson, and "Lambert" Robinson (5 Dec 1800; DB 10/213) sold to Claudius Bailey. It eventually came into the hands of Joseph Caldwell; Caldwell "devised" it to William Hooper, and Hooper sold it (14 Feb 1839; DB 28/414) to Anna Watson, daughter of William Watson, who according to the deed "has been living there." It was still owned by "Ann" Watson on 17 Aug 1857 (DB 35/301).

Lot IV [East side of the Grand Avenue across from 4-acre lot III, north of Rosemary Street and extending north approximately to the line of present North Street]. The Trustees (16 Oct 1793; DB 6/436) sold it to William Hays for £50 5s. Hay[e]s divided the lot into four quarters by lines running north from Rosemary Street, parallel to the Grand Avenue. He sold (17 Apr 1795; DB 5/261) to Thomas Stokes the western quarter, "Begining at a stake on the Southwest side of Lott or square number four (4)...runing a long the south side of the Narrow street [Rosemary] lying on the North side of Franklin street. to a Stake on Gray Barbeys [*sic*] line thence a long said Line to a stake thence West a long the line of said Lot to a Stake, thence South with the line of the Grand Space or Avenue to the begining." On the same day Hay[e]s sold the adjoining strip to the east (17 April 1795; DB 5/500) to Gray Barbee and the third strip to the east (17 Apr 1795; DB 6/391) to George Daniel, who sold it (28 Feb 1798; DB 6/432) to James Trice, who in turn sold it (4 Jan 1802; DB 10/188) to Joseph Trice. Hayes (14 Oct 1800; DB 11/23) sold the fourth (eastern) quarter to Samuel Hopkins, described as the "westward" [*sic*, in error for "eastward"] end of a 4-acre lot, no. 4 on the town plan: bordered on the west by a one-acre lot sold by Hayes to George Daniel, on the north and east by the lands of the Trustees, on the south by a small street [Rosemary]. All the quarters except that owned by Stokes had been sold and resold by 1817 (DB 12/107, 12/125, 13/160, 15/133, 16/96, 18/160, 18/193, 19/185).

Lot V [East side of Hillsborough Street, between Rosemary and North Streets]. The Trustees (18 Oct 1793; DB 5/58–59) sold to John Grant Rencher, for £37 5s, the 4-acre lot "North of the Grand Avenue and numbered (5) five in the plan of said Town." Rencher (14 Aug 1799; DB 8/183) sold to Augustus [Augustine] Benton. Benton (11 Mar 1817; DB 16/44) sold to Joseph Caldwell. We do not know Caldwell's disposition of the lot, but John Neal (30 Aug 1825; DB 21/547–548) sold it to John McGee, "in or near the North eastern extremity of said Village," together with "two Beds, Bedsteads & furniture also two Ropes & Mattrasses for said Bedsteads." (The record also seems to show that John Lewis [20 Apr 1828; DB 23/270] sold the same lot to John McGee.) McGee (20 Feb 1829; DB 23/512) sold it to Elisha Mitchell, and Mitchell (4 Nov 1833; DB 25/478) sold it to Jones Watson. For subsequent history of the lot, see DB 25/479, 33/448.

Lot VI [Referred to by Kemp P. Battle (Battle, 1907) as the "Battle Lot," surrounded by University property, with its eastern boundary in line with those of 2-acre lots 23 and 24, thus approximately at present Boundary Street, and its southern boundary approximately on the north side of present Cameron Avenue, and in line with the southern boundaries of 2-acre lots 1 and 2]. The Trustees (19 Oct 1793; DB 5/89A, copied in 5/368) sold it for £75 to Andrew Burk[e], who sold it less than a year later (29 Aug 1794; DB 5/362) to Robert Donaldson. Archibald D. Murphey (25 Aug 1801; DB 9/261) acquired it by sheriff's sale, and shortly thereafter (3 Sep 1801; DB 10/20) sold it to Thomas Scott. In the next fifty years, often described as "adjacent to the buildings of the university," it passed into the hands of at least a dozen more owners, including (in Mitchell's days) Abner W. Clopton (24 Mar 1814; DB 17/204), William Hooper (21 May 1819; DB 18/73), and Shepard K. Kollock (26 Feb 1822; DB 19/285). After at least seven more owners it was sold by Kendal Waitt and David Swain (22 Jul 1843; DB 33/537) to William H. Battle. Battle subsequently (28 Jan 1845; DB 33/530) bought from the Trustees a further lot of 2 acres, described as 210 by 420 feet on the sides, immediately adjacent (on the south) to his lot VI.

LITERATURE CITED

Elisha Mitchell's books were sold at auction after his death, and many of them were bought by the University of North Carolina. It seems probable that, as one of us has already suggested (M. R. McVaugh, 1987), as the Mitchell volumes nearly doubled the library's holdings at the time, a special stamp, **University Library, N.C.**, was made up for them when they were received. The list below includes comments on some volumes, and information on the stamps found in the UNC Library's copies of Mitchell's references.

Barton, W. P. C. 1815. Florae philadelphicae prodromus. pp. [i]–vii, [9]–100. Philadelphia, 1815.

———. 1817-1818. Vegetable materia medica of the United States. 8 volumes, including *pl. 1–50*. Philadelphia, 1817–1818.

———. 1818. Compendium florae philadelphicae. Vol. 1. pp.[1–viii], [1]–251. Vol. 2. [1]–234. Philadelphia, 1818.

———. 1820-1824. A flora of North America. 3 volumes, including *pl. 1–106*. Philadelphia, 1820–1824. [Vol. 1 of the UNC library copy is stamped **E.Mitchell**].

Battle, Kemp P. 1907, 1912. History of the University of North Carolina. Vol. 1, 1789–1868. pp. [i]–[x], [1]–880. Raleigh, N.C., 1907. Vol. 2, 1868–1912. pp. [i]–[x], [1]–875. 1912.

Beck, Lewis Caleb. 1833. Botany of the northern and middle states. pp. [i]–lv, [1]–471. Albany, N.Y, 1833. [Mitchell cited Beck in a note dated May 1837].

Berkeley, Edmund, & Dorothy Smith Berkeley. 1986. A Yankee botanist in the Carolinas The Reverend Moses Ashley Curtis, D.D. (1808–1872). pp. [1]–242. J. Cramer, Berlin-Stuttgart, 1986.

Bigelow, Jacob. 1814. Florula bostoniensis. pp. [i]–viii, [1]–268. Boston, 1814. [The UNC library copy is stamped **E.Mitchell**].

———. 1817-1821. 1. American medical botany. 6 parts in 3 vols., *pl. 1–60*. Boston, 1817–1821. [The library copy of vol. 1, part 1 is stamped **University Library, N.C.**]

Bridel, Samuel-Elisée de. 1797-1818. Muscologia recentiorum. 2 volumes and 4 supplements. Gotha, Paris, 1797–1818. [The library copy, presumably the one used by Mitchell, is stamped in both volumes **University Library, N.C.**].

Catesby, Mark. 1730-1732, 1734-1747. The natural history of Carolina, Florida and the Bahama Islands. Vol. 1. pp. [i–vi], 1–100, 1–2. *pl. 1–100*. London, 1730–1732. Vol. 2. pp. i–xii, i–xliv, 1–120, 1–2. *pl. 1–100*, appendix *pl. 1–20*. 1734–1747.

Clewell, John Henry. 1902. History of Wachovia in North Carolina. pp. [i]–xiv, 1–365. illus., maps. Doubleday, Page & Company, New York, 1902.

Croom, Hardy Bryan. 1837a. A catalogue of plants native or naturalized in the vicinity of New Bern, North Carolina; with remarks and synonyms. pp. i–x, [3]–52. New York, 1837. [pp. i–x comprise a preface and obituary notice by John Torrey, who read the final proofs after learning of Croom's death by shipwreck. The library copy is stamped **University Library, N.C.**].

———. 1837b. Observations on the genus *Sarracenia*; with an account of a new species. Ann. Lyc. Nat. Hist. N.Y. 4: [95]– 104. 1 colored plate. 1837. [Reprinted with unchanged pagination, new title page].

Croom, Hardy Bryan, & H[arris] Loomis. 1833. Catalogue of plants, observed in the neighbourhood of New Bern, N.C. pp. [1–3], 4–13, [14–15], 16. New Bern, 1833. [M.A. Curtis's copy, presented by Croom. Pages 14–16 are devoted to a list of "organic remains" (shells, bones, and teeth) found in nearby marl pits].

Curtis, Moses Ashley. 1843. An account of some new and rare plants of North Carolina. Amer. J. Sci. 44:80-84. 1843. [The article is dated, "Hillsborough, N. C., Nov. 1, 1842.]

———. 1860. Geological and natural history survey of North Carolina, part III, Botany: containing a catalogue of the plants of the state, with descriptions and history of the trees, shrubs, and woody vines. [i–v], 6, [vii]–viii, [ix], x–xvii, [xviii–xix], 20–123, [124, errata]. Raleigh, 1860. [This volume treats only woody plants. Pages 91–92, on *Benzoin melissaefolium*, "I am indebted to Dr. McRee [James F. McRee, of Wilmington, N.C.] and Prof. Mitchell for my knowledge of this species"].

———. 1867. Geological and natural history survey of North Carolina, part III, Botany; containing a catalogue of the indigenous and naturalized plants of the state. [i–vii], 8–155, [156, omissa, errata]. Raleigh, 1867. [Treats the entire flora as far as known, including cryptogams. Eight species are included in the catalogue on Mitchell's authority].

Dewey, Chester. 1845. Caricography. Amer. J. Sci. 48: 140-144. 1 colored plate. 1845.

Eaton, Amos. 1818. A manual of botany for the northern states. Ed. 2. [1]–[12], 1–524. Albany, N.Y., 1818. [The second edition was corrected and much enlarged over the edition of 1817. A third edition was published in 1822. There was no copy of Eaton's manual among the books in Mitchell's library at his death, but the work is mentioned occasionally in Mitchell's botanical notes, and presumably he had access to it].

Elliott, Stephen. 1816-1821, 1821-1824. A sketch of the botany of South-Carolina and Georgia. Vol. 1. pp. 1–606, [i]–vi. *pl. 1–6*. 1816–1821. Vol. 2. pp. [1]–743, [i]–viii. *pl. 7–12*. Charleston, 1821–1824.

Harshberger, John H. 1899. The botanists of Philadelphia and their work. [i]–xii, [1]–457. *pl. 1–48*. Philadelphia, 1899.

Henderson, Archibald. 1949. The campus of the first state university. frontisp., [i]–xvi, [1–4], 5–412. illus., maps. Chapel Hill, 1949.

Keeney, Elizabeth B. 1992. The botanizers. Amateur scientists in nineteenth-century America. [i]–xii, 1–206. University of North Carolina Press, Chapel Hill, 1992.

McVaugh, Michael R. 1984. Elisha Mitchell's library as an index to his scientific interests. J. Elisha Mitchell Sci. Soc. 100: 50–56. 1984.

———. 1987, 1990. Elisha Mitchell's books and the University of North Carolina library. [Part 1]. Bookmark 55: 27–54. 1987. Part 2. Bookmark 56: 31–70. 1990.

Literature cited

Mears, James A. 1981. Guide to plant collectors represented in the herbarium of the Academy of Natural Sciences of Philadelphia. Proc. Acad. Nat. Sci. Philadelphia 133: 141–165. 1981.

Michaux, André. 1801. Histoire des chênes de l'Amérique. pp. [i, iii], [1]–[56]. *pl.1–36*. Paris, 1801.

———. 1803. Flora boreali-americana. Vol. 1. pp. [i]–[1]–330. *pl. 1–29*. Vol. 2. pp. [i, iii], [1]–340. *pl. 30–51*. Paris, 1803.

Michaux, François André. 1817-1819. The North American sylva. 3 volumes in 7 "half-volumes", including 156 plates. Philadelphia, Paris, 1817–1819. [Mitchell referred at least once to "Michaux Sylva". We have not located a copy that he could have seen].

Mitchell, Elisha. 1842. Elements of geology, with an outline of the geology of North Carolina for the use of the students of the university. pp. [3]–141. map. (place of publication not stated). 1842.

[———]. N. d. Natural history. pp. 1-28. (without stated date, or place of publication); same title, identical wording, different printing. pp. 1–27. (without date or place).

Muhlenberg, Gotthilf Henry Ernest. 1817. Descriptio uberior graminum. pp. [i]–ii, [1]–295. Philadelphia, 1817. [See also **Willdenow**].

Nuttall, Thomas. 1818. The genera of North American plants. Vol. 1. pp. [i]–viii, [1]–312. Vol. 2, pp. [1]–254, index [1]–10, err. [1–4]. Philadelphia, 1818.

Persoon, Christiaan Hendrik. 1805-1807. Synopsis plantarum. Vol. 1. pp. [l]–xii, [1]–546. Paris & Tübingen, 1805. Vol. 2, part 1. pp. [i], [1]–272. 1806. Vol. 2, part 2. pp. [i–iv], 273–657, [err.1–2]. 1807.

Phelps, Almira H. Lincoln. 1853. Familiar lectures on botany. frontisp. [map], [1]-297; appendix, indexes, [1]-208. New ed., revised and enlarged, New York, 1853.

Pursh, Frederick Traugott. 1816. Flora americae septentrionalis. Ed. 2. Vol. 1. pp. [i]–xxxvi, [1]–358. *pl. 1–16*. Vol. 2. pp.[i–ii], [359]–751. *pl. 17–24*. London, 1816. [The "2nd edition" was a reissue of the 1814 edition, with the same printing errors. Mitchell's annotated copy bears the **University Library, N.C.** stamp in both volumes].

Radford, A. E., et al. 1968. Manual of the vascular flora of the Carolinas. pp. lvi, 1183. Univ. of North Carolina Press, Chapel Hill, 1968.

Rees, Abraham. 1806-1818. The cyclopaedia; or, universal dictionary. American edition, 83 parts in 41 volumes. Philadelphia, 1806–1818. [Botanical articles cited by Mitchell were written by James Edward Smith].

Schweinitz, Lewis D. de. 1822. Attempt of a monography of the Linnean genus *Viola*, comprising all the species hitherto observed in North America. Amer. J. Sci. 5: 48–81. Jun 1822. [The author's address was given in the heading as Salem, North Carolina. An editorial footnote states that the manuscript was received July 28, 1821, and says of the author, "Now (April 1822) of Bethlehem, Penn."]

———. 1824. An analytical table to facilitate the determination of the hitherto observed North American species of the genus *Carex*. Ann. Lyc. Nat. Hist. N.Y. 1, part 1: 62–71. 1824. [Here Schweinitz described at least 18 new species of *Carex*].

——— **& John Torrey.** [1826] A monograph of the North American species of *Carex*. Ann. Lyc. Nat. Hist. N.Y. 1, part 2: 283–[374]. *pl. 24–28 Fig. 1, 28 Fig. 2.* "Dec 1825" [1826].

Shear, C. L., & Neil E. Stevens, eds. 1921. The correspondence of Schweinitz and Torrey. Mem. Torrey Bot. Club 16: 119–300. *pl. 6–7.* 1921.

Small, John K. 1933. Manual of the southeastern flora. pp. [i]–xxii, [1]–1554. New York, 1933.

Smith, James Edward. See **Rees.**

Sprengel, Kurt. 1807. Introduction to the study of cryptogamous plants. pp. [i–v], vi–vii, [1]–411. *pl. I–X.* London, 1807. [On the front flyleaf, in pencil, "Prof. Mitchell"; on the title-page, **University Library, N.C.**].

Stafleu, Frans A., & Richard S. Cowan. 1985. Taxonomic literature. Ed. 2. 5: pp. 1–1066. (Regnum vegetabile vol. 112). Utrecht, 1985. [L.D. v. Schweinitz, pp. 437–442].

Stuckey, Ronald L. 1979. Type specimens of flowering plants from eastern North America in the herbarium of Lewis David von Schweinitz. Proc. Acad. Nat. Sci. Philadelphia 131: 9–51. 1979.

Torrey, John. 1819. A catalogue of plants, growing spontaneously within thirty miles of the City of New York. pp. [i]–v, [vii–viii], [9]–100, [101]. Lyc. Nat. Hist. N.Y., Albany, 1819.

———. 1823-1824. A flora of the northern and middle sections of the United States. Vol. 1 only, in 3 parts. pp. [1]–518, [i]–xii. New York, 1823-1824. [With stamp, **University Library, N.C.** and, inside the back cover, pencilled notes in Mitchell's hand].

Vickers, James. 1985. Chapel Hill: An illustrated history. pp. [i–v], 6–208. Barclay Publishers, Chapel Hill, 1985.

Willdenow, Carl Ludwig. 1805, 1806. Species Plantarum. 6 volumes. Berlin, 1797–1825. Vol. 4. pp. [1]–629. 1805 and pp. [631]–1157. 1806. [Numerous names for species of *Carex* attributed to G.H.E. Muhlenberg were published in this volume, and Mitchell's references to Willdenow with respect to *Carex* are presumably based on the same volume. The Pteridophytes, to some of which Mitchell also referred, were published in volume 5. The copies that Mitchell used have not been located].

——— 1811. The principles of botany and of vegetable physiology. new and enlarged ed. pp. [i–viii], [i]–iv, [1]–544, *pl. 1–11.* Edinburgh, London, 1811. [a translation from Grundriss der Kräuterkunde, Berlin, 1792 and later editions. "E. Mitchells Book" is pencilled on the flyleaf in the UNC library copy].

PLANT-NAMES MENTIONED IN THE TEXT

English (common) names mentioned incidentally are not indexed. Page-numbers in **boldface** are of special interest. Modern equivalents for generic names and specific epithets used by Mitchell have not been supplied except in a few instances.

Acer
  rubrum, 50, 55
  not rubrum, 49
Achillea millefolium, 43
Aconitum uncinatum, 47
Actinomeris squarrosa, 62
Aesculus, 36
  flava, 36
  pavia, 36
Agrimonia eupatoria, 45
Agrostemma githago, 40
Agrostis
  brevifolia/spadicea, 12
  spadicea, 13
Aira [Trisetum–Eds.]
  melicoides, 19, 50
  triflora, 19, 50
Aletris alba, 44
algae, freshwater, 6 (studied by Schweinitz)
Allium canadense, 39
Alnus, 55, 56
  serrulata, 49, 54, 55
Amaranthus hybridus, 45
Amaryllis atamasco, 34
Amygdalus
  persica, 32, 54 ("peach blossoms")
  persicaria [sic], 50
Andromeda, 40
  mariana, 39
  nitida, 11, 12
  paniculata, 41
  racemosa, 37
  speciosa nitida, 41
  speciosa ?, var. pulverulenta, 41
Andropogon, 53

Anemone, a new species, 35
  lancifolia, 34
  nemorosa, 34, 35
  thalictroides, 24, 33
  virginica, 43
Angelica, 39
  lucida, 39
Antirrhinum, 67
  canadense, 31
Aphyllon uniflorum, 13
Apios frutescens, 47
Apocynum
  cannabinum, 41
  pubescens, 41
Arabis, 22
  falcata, 39
  lyrata, 19, 23, 24, 50
  rhomboidea, 54
  thaliana, 34
Arctium lappa, 57
Arenaria squarrosa, 20
Aronia, 33, 34
Arum [=Arisaema–Eds.]
  dracontium, 40
  triphyllum, 19, 40, 50, 80
Asarum
  arifolium, 12, 24, 33
  virginicum, 24, 33
Asclepias, 41
  amplexicaulis, 43
  angustifolia, 13
  lanceolata, 42
  linifolia, 12
  mitchelii, 12
  obovata, 42
  variegata, 40

Asclepias
    verticillata-angustifolia, 12
    viridiflora obovata, 42
Asplenium ebeneum, 41
Aster, **26**, 53, 61
    conyzoides, 43
    ericoides, 45, 48
    patens, 61
    phlogifolius, 47
    puniceus, 44
Azalea, 36
    canescens, 12
    nudiflora, 37
    periclymenoides, 37
    viscosa, 41
Baccharis, 12
    glomieruliflora [sic], 12
Barbarea vulgaris, 54
Bartramia pomiformis, 53
Bartsia coccinea, 44
Benzoin melissaefolium, 13, 26, 108
Bidens bipinnata, 45,
Bignonia
    capreolata, 39
    radicans, 44
Bletia aphylla, 54
Bromus secalinus, 42
Bryum, 56
Bumelia, 12
Bupleurum rotundifolium, 12
Cacalia ("Calcalia") atriplicifolia, 43
Cactus opuntia, 50
Callitriche heterophylla, 34
Caprifolium sempervirens, 36
Cardamine
    ludoviciana, 13
    pennsylvanica [pennsylvaniana], 32, 57
    virginica, 23, 32, 55
Carex, 6, 8, 13, 19, 20, **26–28**, 50, **55**, 56, **58–61**, 110
    acuta, 59
    anceps, 59
    brizoides, 27, 61
    caespitosa, 59
    canescens, 27, 60
    cephalophora ?, 61
    conoidea ?, 59, 60
    crinita, 60
    curta, 27, 60
    digitalis ?, 59
    elongata, 27, 60
    festucacea, 26, 27, 55, 59, 60
    folliculata, 60

Carex
    hirsuta, 57, 59
    laxiflora, 59
    loliacea, 27, 60
    marginata, 59
    miliacea, 57, 60
    mitchelliana, 13, **61**
    multiflora, 54, 59
    retroflexa, 59
    scoparia, 27, 60, 61
    sempervirens, 11
    squarrosa, 60
    straminea, 27, 60
    tentaculata, 60
    varia, 58, 59
    willdenowii ?, 60
Carpinus, 35
    americana, 50
Cassia
    chamaecrista, 45
    marylandica, 47
    nictitans, 45
Castanea
    chinquapin, 43
    vesca, 43
Centaurea calcitrapa, 13
Cerastium, 50
Cerastium glutiniosum [sic], 36
Cercis canadensis, 33
Chaerophyllum [=Osmorhiza–Eds.], 22, 23
    claytoni, 19, 23, 24, 50
Chaptalia tomentosa, 11
Chelone glabra, 47
Chenopodium
    anthelminticum, 47
    botrys, 45
Chimaphila ("Chimiphila") maculata, 43
Cicuta maculata, 39, 40
Cineraria ?, 39, 40
Claytonia virginica, 24, 33
Clematis
    holosericea, 46
    virginica, 46
Clitoria
    mariana, 44
    virginiana, 45
Cnicus
    lanceolatus, 44
    muticus, 47
Conyza camphorata, 46
Coreopsis
    auriculata, 37
    verticillata, 43

Cornus
  caroliniana, 12, 13
  didyma, 12
  sericea, 41
Corrallorhiza [sic], 57
Corydalis aurea, 57
Corylus, 56
  americana, 54
Crataegus, 51, 56
  apiifolia, 51
  coccinea, 52
  crus galli, 52
  parvifolia, 39, 52
  pyrifolia, 37, 51, 80
  spathulata, 39, 52
Croomia, 17
Crotolaria [sic] sagittalis, 44
Cuphaea [sic] viscosissima, 44
Cymbidium pulchellum, 41
Cypripedium, 44
Dalibarda fragarioides, 35
Datura, 23
Dentaria
  heterophylla, 24, 33
  tenella, 33
Diodia, 44
Dioscorea villosa, 39
Diospyros virginiana, 40
Dolichos, 61
Draba, 7
  hispidula, 21, 49, 50, 54, 56
  verna, 7, 49, 50, 54–56
Dracocephalum
  denticulatum, 46
  virginianum, 46
Eclipta ["Eclipsa"], 12
  erecta, 12 ["Eclipsa"], 47
  procumbens, 47
Ellisia nyctelea, 13, 19, 22, **23**, 50, 54, 80
Epigaea repens, 24, 32
Erigeron, 8
  canadense, 45
  heterophyllum, 40
  nudicaule, 11
  strigosum, 39
Erysimum barbarea, 54
Erythronium [also "Erithronium",
    "Erythronum"], 55 ["not yet out"]
  americanum, 24, 32
  lanceolatum, 32, 50, 54
Euonymus
  americanus, 38
  atropurpureus, 13
Eupatorium, 46

Eupatorium
  album, 45
  altissimum, 47
  falcatum, 45
  linearifolium, 47
  parviflorum, 12, 13
  purpureum, 46
  rotundifolium, 44
Euphorbia, a new species ?, 34
  portulaccoides, 38
Fedia radiata, 39
ferns, 20, 41, 43, 40 (see also individual
    species)
Ferula villosa, 43
fungi, 6 (in Schweinitz's herbarium), 13
    (in M.A. Curtis's herbarium)
Galactia mollis, 44
Galium
  aparine, 38
  circaezans, 42
  uniflorum, 38
gama grass, 16
Gelsemium nitidum, 34,
Gentiana saponaria, 53
Geranium maculatum, 37
Gerardia, 53
  flava, 44
  quercifolia, 46, 47
Geum virginianum, 43
Gnaphalium, 7
  germanicum, 47
  plantagineum, 34
  uliginosum, 42
Gonolobus
  hirsutus, 42
  hispidus, 42
  macrophyllus, 42
Gratiola, 37
  acuminata, 47
  sphaerocarpa, 55
  virginica, 37
Grimmia
  apicola, 54
  controversa, 54
Hedysarum [=Desmodium–Eds.], 26, **48**
  bracteosum, 48
  canescens, 48
  ciliare, 48
  glabellum, 48
  nudiflorum, 44, 48
  obtusum, 48
  paniculatum, 46, 48
  rotundifolium, 48
  viridiflorum, 45, 48

Helenium autumnale, 46
Helianthus, 46
   atrorubens, 46
   decapetalus, 46
   macrophyllus, 46
   tomentosus, 12
Heliopsis laevis, 46
Heliotropium indicum, 45
Helonias
   angustifolia, 11
   dioica, 38
   erythrosperma ?, 40
Hepaticae, 7, 43 [see also Liverworts]
Hepatica triloba, 24, 32, 54
Heuchera
   americana, 38
   viscida, 38
Hexastylis, 24
   minor, 24
Hieracium
   gronovii (foliosum), 45
   venosum, 30, 36
Hopaea tinctoria, 11
Houstonia
   caerulea, 54
   purpurea, 38
Hypericum corymbosum, 44
Hypnum, 56
   minutulum, 53
   riparioides, 53
Hypoxis
   erecta, 19, 36, 50
   graminea, 36
Hyssopus nepetoides, 46
Ilex, 40, 42, 51
   prinoides, 37, 40
Inula
   argentea, 46
   graminifolia, 46
   mariana, 47
Iris cristata, 36
Isanthus coeruleus, 43
Itea virginica, 40
Juglans
   porcina, 48
   tomentosa, 48
Juncus effusus, 41
Justicia
   brachiata, 12
   pedunculosa, 43
Kalmia latifolia, 40
Krigia, 42
   virginica, 36
Lactuca elongata, 43

Lamium amplexicaule, 35
Lathyrus venosus, 34
Laurus, 25
   benzoin, 25, 32
   caroliniensis, 20
   diospyrus ["diospyros"], 12, 25, 33, 81
   geniculata, 25, 54, 81
   melisoides, 12
   melissifolia, 11
   sassafras, 32
Leonurus, 56
   cardiaca, 57
Leskea, 56
Lespedeza
   capitata, 46
   polystachya, 46
   sessiliflora, 46
Liatris, 46, **62**, 80
   aspera, 62
   bellidifolia, 20
   cylindracea, 62
   elegans, 62
   gracilis, 62
   graminifolia, 12, 62
   heterophylla, 62
   macrostachya ?, 62
   pilosa, 62
   pycnostachya, 62
   resinosa, 62
   scariosa, 62
   secunda, 62
   sphaeroidea, 62
   squarrosa, 46, 62
   tenuifolia, 62
lichens, 6 [studied by Schweinitz]
Lindera
   benzoin, 25
   melissifolia, 11, **25–26**
Linum virginicum, 44
Lithospermum, 19, 50
   arvense, 35
liverworts, 6, 7 [studied by Schweinitz].
   See also Hepaticae
Lobelia
   amoena, 31
   cardinalis, 46
   cliffortiana ?, 42
Ludwigia
   decurrens, 44
   lucida, 42
   palustris, 42
Lupinus
   perennis, 11
   villosa, 11

Lycopodium apodum, 7, 43
Lycopus virginicus, 45
Lysimachia, 42
    ciliata, 40, 42
    heterophylla ?, 42
    quadrifolia, 41
Magnolia
    acuminata, 38
    tripetala, 38
Marchantia polymorpha, 7, 43
Marrubium vulgare, 41
Melanthium virginicum, 44
Melica glabra, 57
Menispermum canadense lobatum, 41
Mikania scandens, 45
Mimulus
    alatus, 44
    ringens, 47
Mnium, 56
    cuspidatum, 56
Mollugo verticillata, 44
Monarda
    clinopodia, 12
    mollis, 63
Monotropa
    lanuginosa, 43
    morisoniana, 47
    uniflora, 47
Morus rubra, 37
mosses, 6, 8, 20, 29, 49, 50, 53, 54, **56**
Myosotis arvensis, 19, 50
Narcissus pseudo-narcissus, 31
Nemophila aphylla, 23
Neottia pubescens, 57
Nicandra physaloides, 12
oaks, in Michaux's work, 20
Oenothera
    fruticosa, 39
    hybrida, 39
    muricata, 44
    sinuata, 39
Onosmodium hispidum, 40
Orchis
    ciliaris, 44
    psycodes, 44
Orobanche uniflora, 54
Orontium aquaticum, 19, **25**, 33, 50, 80
Osmorhiza [see also Chaerophyllum]
    longistylis, 24
Osmunda spectabilis, 43
Ostrya, 35
    virginica, 50
Oxalis
    corniculata, 19, 34, 50

Oxalis
    dillenii, 44
    lyoni, 34
    violacea, 34
Panax trifolium, 54
Panica floribus diffusis solitariis, 58
Panicum, 26, **55**, **57–58**
    ciliatum, 58
    ensifolium, 55
    latifolium, 58
    nitidum, 58
    pauciflorum, 58
    pubescens, 58
    strigosum, 58
    villosum, 58
Paspalum
    floridanum, 53
    strictum, 12
Passiflora lutea, 39, 45
Pedicularis canadensis, 19, 34, 50, 80
Penstemon, 33
Penstimon [sic] laevigata, 39
Penthorum sedoides, 44
Phaseolus, 48
    helvolus, 61
    perennis, 48
    vexillatus, 61
Phleum pratense, 42
Phlox, **37**
    acuminata, 12, 37
    amoena, 37
    aristata, 33, 37, 52
    carolina, 37
    cordata, 37
    divaricata, 37
    glaberrima, 37, 38
    maculata ("maculalata"), 37, 44
    nitida, 37, 50
    paniculata, 37
    pilosa, 37, 52
    pyramidalis, 37
    reptans, 37
    setacea, 21, 62
    suaveolens, 37
    subulata, 21, 33, 62
    undulata, 37
Phryma leptostachia, 44
Physalis, 40, **41**
    lanceolata, 52
    obscura. 41
    pubescens, 41, 52
    viscosa, 41
Pinguicula
    elatior, 11

Pinus
  inops, 35
  variabilis, 48
Poa, 26, **51**
  annua, 21, 50, 51
  autumnalis, 55
  stolonifera, 51
  stricta (sp. nov. ined.), 51
  viridis, 55
Poae, 51
Podalyria villosa, 11
Podophyllum peltatum, 33
Polygala
  alba, 37
  albida, 37
  incarnata, 42
  senega, 37
  verticillata, 43
Polygonatum angustifolium, 38
Polygonum
  mite, 45
  virginianum, 47
Polymnia uvedalia, 45
Polypodium hexagonopterum, 43
Polytrichum
  perigoniale, 53
  undulatum, 49, 53
Potamogeton, 54
Potentilla simplex, 19, 36, 50
Prenanthes, 61, **62**
  alba, 62, 82
  altissima, 62
  cordata, 62
  crepidinea, 62
  juncea, 62
  rubicunda, 62
  serpentaria, 62
  simplex, 62
  virgata, 62
Prinus, 42
  verticillata ?, 42
Prunella pennsylvanica, 40
Prunus, 35, 50
  chicasa, 8, 31, 32, 50, 54 ("the red plum")
  serotina, 36
  virginiana, 36
Psoralea mellilotoides, 42
Ptelea trifoliata, 53, 78
Pteris aquilina, 41
Pycnanthemum, 43
  aristatum, 53
  incanum, 44, 53

Pyrus
  alnifolia, 34
  botryapium, 33
  melanocarpa, 34
  ovalis, 34
Quercus, 20, 26, **52**
  alba, 52
  aquatica, 48, 53
  coccinnea [sic], 52
  falcata, 52
  lyrata, 53
  nigra, 48, 52
  obtusifolia, 52, 67
  phellos, 53
  prinus discolor, 52
  prinus monticola, 53
  prinus palustris, 53
  rubra, 53
  tinctoria, 52
Ranunculus, 8, 22, 37, **51**, 56
  abortivus, 22, 34, 57
  acris, 51
  auricomus, 51
  bulbosus, 63
  fascicularis, 22, 23, 36, 56, **57**, 62
  hirsutus, 22, 57
  hispidus, 23
  lanuginosus, 21, 51
  nitidus, 22, 23, 57
  recurvatus, 21, 35, 50, 51
  sceleratus, 22, 57
  tomentosus, 51
red plum, 54
Rhexia mariana rubella, 44
Rhododendron, 79, 82
  catawbiense, 25, 81
  maximum, 25, 38
  punctatum, 25, 38
  roseum, 25, 38
Rosa, 41
Rubus
  flagellaris, 36
  trivialis, 36
Rudbeckia digitata, 46
Ruellia, 40
Sabbatia
  angularis, 44
  chloroides, 12
  corymbosa, 44
Salix, 8, **56**
Salvia
  lyrata, 31
  urticifolia, 38

Samolus valerandi, 40
Sanguinaria canadensis, 20, 24, 33
Sarracenia, 16
   flava, 11
   purpurea, 11
Sassafras albidum, 25
Sassafras, odor of in Asarum, 24, 33
Saururus cernuus, 44
Saxifraga, 55
   vernalis, 32
   virginiensis, 24, 32, 50, 54
Scirpus capitatus, 54
Scorzonera pinnatifida, 42
Scrophularia marylandica, 41
Scutellaria
   integrifolia, 42
   lateriflora, 46
   serrata, 38
sedges, 20
Senecio, 40
   balsamitae, 40
Shad Flower, 33
Sibara virginica, 23
Sida
   abutilon, 47
   spinosa, 44
Silene
   antirrhina, 38
   virginica, 40
Silphium, 46
   laciniatum, 12
Sisyrinchium [see also Sysirinchium]
   anceps, 36
   gladiatum, 36
Sium tricuspidatum, 47
Smilacina racemosa, 37
Smilax
   herbacea, 38
   rotundifolia, 37
Smyrnium
   aureum, 34, 54
   cordatum, 34
   integerrimum, 40
   trifoliatum, 34
Solidago, 26, 53
   aspera, 26
   bicolor, 26
   latifolia, 45
   odora, 26
   patula, 48
   procera, 47
   sorbifolia, 12
   virgata, 12

Sonchus, 46
   oleraceus, 39
Spergula saginoides, 33
Spermacoce
   diodina, 12, 44
   tenuior, 12
   tenuis, 12
Spiraea
   aruncus, 38
   trifoliata, 38
Stachys
   aspera, 44
   hispida, 44
Staphylea trifolia, 34, 35
Stellaria, 8
   dichotoma, 32
   media, 32
   pubera, 24, 32
Stipa avenacea, 19, 50
Strophostyles peduncularis, 61
Stylosanthes hispida erecta, 7, 43
Styrax glabrum, 11
Symplocos, 11
Sysirinchium [sic] anceps, 19, 50
Taxus, 17
Tephrosia
   hispidula, 46
   virginiana, 40
Teucrium virginicum, 43
Thalictrum rugosum, 39
Thaspium barbinode, 54
Thlaspi bursa pastoris, 56
Tiarella cordifolia, 35, 50
Torreya, 17
Tradescantia virginica, 31
Tragia urticifolia, 43
Trifolium
   arvense, 44
   procumbens. 39
Trillium, 36
   catesbaei, 35, 50
   nervosum, 12
Triosteum angustifolium, 54
Tripsacum
   dactyloides, 16
   monostachyon, 16
Troximon virginicum, 42
Ulmus americana, 49, 55
Uraspermum, 19, 50
Utricularia subulata, 10–11
Uvularia
   flava, 36
   perfoliata, 36, 54

Uvularia
  sessilifolia, 35
Vaccinium, 37, 40
  corymbosum, 32
  stamineum, 36
  tenellum, 34
Verbascum, 23
  blattaria, 40
Verbena
  hastata, 41
  officinalis, 41
  rugosa, 42
  spuria, 41
  urticifolia, 43
Verbesina coreopsis, 62
Vernonia
  fasciculata, 13
  novebor[ac]ensis, 44
Veronica
  arvensis, 35
  peregrina, 33
  serpyllifolia, 35
Viburnum, 19, 37, 38, 50
  nudum, 11
  prunifolium, 33
  pubescens, 12, 36
Viola, 6, 11, 36
  arvensis, 33

Viola
  bicolor, 33
  blanda, 36
  concolor, 54
  cucullata, 32
  digitata, 11
  hastata, 35, 50
  palmata dilatata, 33
  primulifolia, 36
  pubescens, 19, 50
  sagittata, 8, 11, 12
  sagittatta [sic] emarginata, 51
  serpyllifolia, 36
  striata, 19, 50
  tricolor, 56
Virginia creeper, 40
Vitis
  aestivilis [sic], 40
  riparia, 12, 40
Waldsteinia, 35
Wisteria, 47
  speciosa, 47
Xyris caroliniana, 46
Yucca
  angustifolia, 42
  filamentosa, 42
Zanthorr[h]iza apiifolia, 34

PERSONAL NAMES MENTIONED IN THE TEXT

Names of botanical authors mentioned by Elisha Mitchell in his botanical notes are not routinely indexed here, but are fully identified under "Literature Cited". Surnames in [brackets] are alternative spellings, especially those used on land-deeds; it is not always clear which spelling was the preferred one. Names inclosed in quotation marks, as "Barbey", are understood to be mis-spellings, though in the late 18th and early 19th centuries there was considerable latitude in this. Page-numbers in **boldface** indicate special significance for the item in question. The name of Elisha Mitchell is on almost every page, and is not indexed except when it appears in land-transactions. In the section devoted to botanical notes (pages 29–63), the most frequently occurring personal names attached to Mitchell's botanizing localities (e.g. "Merits Meadow"), are not routinely indexed.

Adams, John, 100
Anderson Blackwood & Co., 101
Anderson, Christiane, 2
Andersons corner, 96
Arnott, Dr.[G. A. W.], 17
Ashe, Anna [L.], 101
Ayers surveying files, 72
Bailey, Claudius, 105
Baldwin, William, 15
Barbee [Barbey], Gray, 106
Barbee, Christopher, 39, 51 [both Barbees Plantation], 53 [Barbees Eastern Mill], 54 [Barbees on Bollings Creek], 65, **69**, **75**, **86**, 99, **105**
Barbee, Delia, 76
Barbee, Old Mr., 54, 75
Barbee, William, 65, 66, 75, 90, 96, 99
Barbey, Barby, see Barbee
Bartram, John, 15
Battle, Kemp P., 3, 106 ["the Battle Lot"]
Battle, William H., 106
Benton, Augustus [Augustine], 102, 103, 106
Benton, Frances, 103
Bevill [Bevil], Elisha, 57, 68, **75**, 79
Blake's line, 102
Blake, Charles, 95

Blake, S. F., 10
Bolin [Bowlin], Benjamin, 75
Booth [Boothe], Daniel, 100, 101
Bruederle, Leo P., 2, 13, 61
Burk [Burke], Andrew, **105**, 106
Caldwell, J., 96
Caldwell, John, 66, 99, 104
Caldwell, Joseph (or Dr., Mr., or President), 3–5, 9, 44, 47, 52, 56, 65, 66, **76**, 78, 84, 88, 100, 103–106
Caldwell, Mrs., 42, 67, 76
Campbell, Archibald, **98**
Campbell, Robert, 102, 103
Candolle, A. P. de, 15
Carr, John W., 94, 99
Carrington, James, [Jr.] (son of John), 99
Carrington, John, [Sr.], 99
Cave, Belfield W., 38, **76**
Chamberlain, Faith Summerell, 4
Cherry, Kevin, 2
Child, James, 104
Christmas, Nathaniel, 102
Clopton, Abner W., 66, 67, 106
Cobb, Collier, 98
Collier, Charles, 94, 103
Collier, Frederick, 103
Collier, J. J., 104

Connally, Thomas, 83, **92**
Craig, 39 [beyond Craigs], 40, 42 [Craigs field], 53 [beyond Craigs], 71 [Craig property], 72 [Craig's mill], **77** [Craig property]
Craig, Abraham, 100
Craig, James, **77**, **86**, Map 1
Craig, Jane, 101
Craig, John, 77, 79, 84–86, 96 [plot of a village lot], 100, 104, Map 1
Craig, Mrs. [James], 36 , 47, **77**
Craig, Whitted, 100
Croom, Hardy Bryan, **16–17**, 108
Curtis, Moses Ashley, **13**, 14, 17, 23, 26, 61
Daniel, 57, 59, 72 [map of 1792]
Daniel, George, 106
Daniel, John, 68, **77**, 103
Daniel, John, [Jr.], **89**
Darlington, William, 15, 16
Davie, William R., 101
Denke, C. F., 6
Dewey, Chester, 13, 61
Dixon, John [Joseph], 100
Donaldson, Robert, 106
Durham, William, 90
Eaton, Amos, 17
Edwards, Thomas, 99
Elliott, Stephen, 17
Ewan, Joseph, 2
Felton, Mary McKee, 2
Fetter, Manuel, 104
Forrest, Virginia C., 1
Frazier, Ephraim, 94
Gapins, Stephen, 94
Gillaspie, James S. [James L.], 88, 105
Granville, John, Earl [Lord], 6, 87
Green, William M. [W. M.], 104, 105
Hargis, Mrs., 96
Hatch, Abijah, 104
Hatch, Thomas, 104
Haws [Hawes], Dr. Elias, 65, 99, 103, 103
Hayes [Hays], William, **106**
Haywood, William Henry, 102
Henderson, Alexander, 101
Henderson, Maj. (Major) Pleasant, 36, 37, 40–42, 53–55, 64, 65, 77, **78**, 81, 84, **88**, 96, 100, **101**
Hill, William Henry [W. H.], 94, **103**
Hilliard, 64, 65
Hilliard [Hillyard], Lucy, 105
Hilliard's Hotel [Tavern], 64, 65
Hogan, John, 83, **92**
Hogg, James, 64, 65, 101
Holmes, Samuel Allen, 105
Hooper, John de Berniere, 104
Hooper, 65, 78
Hooper, Mrs., 34, 78
Hooper, William, 3, 65, 66, **78**, **104**, 105, 106
Hopkins, Samuel, 85, **88**, 101, 102, 106
Hunt, William Lanier, 2
Hutchens, John, 101
Hutchins, John, 96
Johnston, George, 85, 101
Jones's Mill, 72; Jones's road, 86
Jones, Col., 53, 54, **78**
Jones, Edmond [Edmund], **79**, 85, **88**, **90**, 94, 102, **105**
Jones, Edward, **90**
Jones-Roe, Charlotte, 2
Jussieu, Antoine-Laurent de, 15
Keeney, Elizabeth, 14
Keyser, [Kay], 77 ["the Keyser house"]
Kimble, John, 102
King, Nathaniel J. [Nathaniel, "N. I."], 96, 100, 101, 105
Kirk, James, **95**
Kirk, John L., 96
Kirk, Lewis, 94, **95**
Kittrell ("Kittrel", or "Kitterell"), Bryant, [most pages from 31–60], 68, 69, 71, 76, **79**, 80, 86,   **90**
Kollock, Shepard K., 3, 66, 106
Leconte, John Eatton, 17
Leconte, Louis, 17
Leigh ["Lee"], James B., 57, 68, **79**
Lewis, Elizabeth (wife of Orren), 96
Lewis, John, 96, 101, 105, 106
Lewis, Mr. [Orrin, Oran, Orran, Orren, Orlan], 8, 32, 38, **79**, **96**, 102
Lincoln, Mrs. (Almira H.), see Phelps.
Linnaeus, Carolus, 15, 21, 22
Lloyd, Stephen, his orphans, 93
Lloyd, Thomas, 93
Long, James, 93
Loomis, Harris, 16
Love, Robert, 84
Love, Samuel, 84
MacBride, James, 17
MacGee house, see McGee
Marshall, Humphry, 15
Mason, Jesse, 100
Mason, Mrs. James P. (Mary Morgan Mason), 89, 90
Mason, William, 104
Massey, J. R., 2
McCauley, 60, 68, 72 (McCauley's Mill), 90
McCauley, John, 99, 100

McCauley, Mathew [Matthew], **79**, 83, 88, **93**, 99, 100
McCauley, William, **79**, **83**, 99
McGee [MacGee], John, 96, 100, 106
McRee, Dr. James F., 108
McVaugh, Julia A., 2
McVaugh, M.R., 11
Mears, James, 11
Mebane, Alexander, 99
Merritt ["Merit"), William Henry [including Merits Meadow, Merits Mill Pond, etc.], [most pages from 33–60], 68, **69**, 79, **80**, **90**, **91**
Mickle, Andrew, 101
Mitchell, Elisha, 65, 66, 76, **80**, 84, **91**, 92, 96, 105, 106
Mitchell, James, 102
Mitchell, Maria (Mrs. Elisha Mitchell), 8, 11, 66
Mitchell, Mrs. (Sarah), 64, 65
Moore, Alfred, 94, 103
Morgan, Hardy, 68, 70, 73, 85, **87**, 88, 101, Map 1
Morgan, John, 85, 89, **90**, **91**
Morgan, Jones, **89**, 90
Morgan, Lemuel, 85
Morgan, Louisa, 89, **90**
Morgan, Mark, 87, 89
Morgan, Mary, 89, **90**
Morgan, Sampson, 89, **90**
Morgan, Sol[omon], 55 [Sol. Morgans land], 90, Map 1
Morgan, Solomon P., 59, **81**, **89**
Morris, Henry, 93
Moseley ["Mosely"], William D., **64–66**
Muhlenberg, G. H. E., 110
Murphey, Archibald D., 106
Musser, Daniel G., 2
Neal, John, 106
Nevill ("Nevell"), Jesse, 102
Norwood, Mr. ("on New Hope"), 37, **80**
Norwood, Walter, 102
Norwood, William, 101
Nunn, David H. (son of William), 65, 99
Nunn, Mrs. William ["Miss"] (Elizabeth), 64, 65, 96, 98
Nunn, William, 85, **98**, 99
Nuting [sic], George, 102
Olmsted, Denison, 3, 9, 14, 57, 65–67, **80**, 104
Pannill, Mrs., 65
Pannill, William, 66, 96 [plot of a village lot], 105
Patterson, Chesley Page, 103, 104
Patterson, James, 85, **98**

Patterson, Mark, 84
Pfaff, Margie, 2
Phelps, Almira H. Lincoln, 15
Phillips, Charles, 104, 105
Phillips, James, 65, 103–105
Piper, 76 ["Piper's house"]
Piper, Alexander, **86**, Map 1
Pitt, Edmund, 65, 100
Pitt, Edmund [sic] R., 102
Pitt, Edward R., 100
Pitts [Pitt], Edmund, 64
Poe, Hasten, 93
Potts, Mr. [Jacob], 63, 78, **84**
Puckett, Elizabeth, 66
Puckett ["Pucket"], Mrs. Jane, 65, 66, 104
Purefoy, 80 [Purefoy's Mill]
Pursh, Frederick, **7**
Putney, James, 84, 100
Radford, Albert E., 2
Ramsay [Ramsey], John A., 65, 100
Reeves, Archibald, 102
Rencher, John Grant, **103**, **106**
Rhodes, Benjamin, 65, 100
Riggsby, Jesse ["Jessey"], 84
Robinson, Lemuel ["Samuel", "Lambert"], 105
Robson, Edward, 100, 104
Schuyler, E. A., 2
Schweinitz, Lewis David de, **6–9**, 10–13, 17, 20, 21, 29, 31, 38, 43, 52, 53
Scott [Scott's Hole], **81**
Scott, Thomas, 106
Short, Charles Wilkins, 11
Smith, Dr. James, 77
Smith, James Edward, 109
Smith, John, 96
Stewart, Pearson, 2
Stokes, Thomas, 106
Stone, Rodman N., 96, 102
Strain, Alexander, 84
Strain, Samuel D., 86
Stubbins, Joseph, 102
Stuckey, R. L., 2, 11
Summerell, Jane, 1
Swain, David, 106
Taylor, John, 65, 86–88, 102, Map 1
Taylor, John, Sr., **81**, 102, 103
Taylor, Mr., 33, 35, 36, 40, 44, 48–50, 54, 55, 59, 67, **81**
Taylor, Thomas H., **81**, 84, 100, 102, 103
Taylor, Tom [Thomas], 64, 65, 94
Thompson, Henry, 94
Thompson, James, 99
Thompson, Joseph, 99
Thompson, Richard, **91**

Thompson, William, 94, 103
Thompsons ground, 100
Torrey, John, 6, 16, 17, 108
Trice, 64
Trice, George W., 65, 99, 103
Trice, Harrison, 65, 103
Trice, James, 106
Trice, Joseph, 106
Trice, William, 65, 103
Van Vleck, Jacob, 6
Waitt, Kendal, 106
Ward, James, 9
Watson, Anna [Ann], daughter of William, 105
Watson, Bennett, 102
Watson, Jones, 106
Watson, [Mr.], 47 [Watsons shop], 65, **81**
Watson, William, 81, 105
Webb, Dr., 47, 78, 81
Webb, [Dr.] James [of Hillsborough], 78, 84, 100, 101
Webb, William Edwards, 105
Weigelt, Christoph, 12
White, Peter S., 2
White, Sheldon, 2
White, William, 103
Whitted, William, 84, 100, 102, Map 1
Whitted & Craig, 84, 100
Whyte, Mr., 62, **82**
Whyte, Thomas E., 82, 103
Yancey ["Yancy"], 99
Yancey, Dr. Charles R., 99, 101
Yarborough, Mr., 44, 47, **78**
Yeargain [Yeargan, Yeargains,], Benjamin, 68, 72 (Yeargains Mill), **84**, 85, **87**, Map 1

Map 1. Chapel Hill and vicinity about as it was when Mitchell first came to the University. The numbered tracts represent individual land-holdings, including those donated to the University Trustees in 1792 and thereafter, the lands of Solomon Morgan (tracts 24–27) that ultimately came into the possession of the University, and some additional tracts that had some significance for Mitchell during his botanizing years, or that he later bought. Boundaries of land-holdings and village lots are in black, streams in blue, and roads in red. The roads are approximately as shown in the Daniel map of 1792.

Where space permits, each tract is identified on the map by number, by owner and date of acquisition, and, in the case of the original donations to the Trustees, by the name of the donor. All the tracts are identified, located, and briefly described in Appendix D. Three tracts (nos. 33–35) that were among the donations to the Trustees are not mapped; none was mentioned or visited by Mitchell as far as we know, and we do not know precisely where any one of them was located.

The following tracts, for want of space on the map, are identified there by number only: no. 5, William Whitted & John Craig 1805; no. 11, Trustees from Alexander Piper 1796; no. 13, Trustees from James Craig 1796; no. 15, Trustees from Benjamin Yeargain 1796; no. 16, Trustees from Hardy Morgan 1793 (by purchase); no. 17, Trustees from Hardy Morgan 1796 (donation); no. 18, John Taylor 1799.

CHA

SHOWING

OTHER RELEVANT

ELIS

MORGAN CREEK

McCAULEY'S MILL

COPYRIGHT PENDING